WILLS FOR ONTARIO

David I. Botnick, LL.B.

Self-Counsel Press
(a division of)
International Self-Counsel Press Ltd.
Canada   U.S.A.

Printed in Canada.

First edition: February 1973
Tenth edition: June 1990
Fifteenth edition: May 1997
Reprinted: September 1997; December 1998

Canadian Cataloguing in Publication Data

Botnick, David I., 1957-
    Wills for Ontario

    (Self-counsel legal series)
    First-9th eds. by Laurence C. Caroe.
    ISBN 1-55180-140-X

    1. Wills — Ontario — popular works. 2. Probate law and
practice — Ontario — Popular works. I. Title II. Series.
KEO287.Z82C37 1997   346.71305'4   C97-910312-6
KF755.Z9C37 1997

Self-Counsel Press
(a division of)
International Self-Counsel Press Ltd.

1481 Charlotte Road   1704 N. State Street
North Vancouver, BC V7J lHl   Bellingham, WA 98225
Canada   U.S.A.

ORDER FORM

Please send me —

_____Have You Made Your Will, $6.95

Please add $3.00 postage to your order and PST and GST to the total.

All prices subject to change without notice.

❑ Money order enclosed for $_____.
❑ Charge to my credit card (see below).

Name _____

Address _____

City _____ Province _____

Postal code _____Telephone_____

MasterCard/Visa number_____

Expiry date_____ Validation date _____

Signature_____

To:

Self-Counsel Press
4 Bram Court
Brampton, ON   L6W 3R6

SCP-WILLONT 15/98

CONTENTS

SAMPLES

NOTICE TO READERS

1
WILLS AND YOUR LAWYER

a. WHAT IS A WILL?

A will is a document prepared by you during your lifetime to take effect upon your death. It directs how the various assets and possessions you own will be disposed of when you die. The person making a will is called a "testator," if a man, and a "testatrix," if a woman. A will must be in writing. It cannot, for example, be dictated into a tape recording machine.

The function of a will is twofold. It directs to whom the assets of a deceased person are to be distributed, and it appoints a person (called an "executor," if a man, and an "executrix," if a woman) to carry out this distribution and other matters involved in the administration of the estate. This person is also known as an "estate trustee."

b. DOES A WILL HAVE ANY EFFECT BEFORE DEATH?

By signing a will, you do not restrict yourself in any way with regard to the disposal of your assets during the rest of your lifetime. In other words, a will is said to "speak" only at the moment of death. In spite of the fact that you may have signed a will leaving your home to your brother, for example, you are perfectly free to sell that home the next day without the consent of your brother. Upon your death, the will would be read as though no gift of the house were contained in it. In short, a person to whom a specific asset is left gets nothing if the asset has already been disposed of. A person who receives money or property under a will is known as a "beneficiary."

c. IS A LAWYER NECESSARY?

There is no legal requirement that a will be prepared by a lawyer. Nor, in many cases, is there any practical need for retaining legal help in the preparation of a will.

Be careful, however, if you intend to draft your own will; the following considerations should be kept in mind:

(a) If you are about to be married, you should probably seek legal advice, for, as will be discussed later, a will made prior to marriage may be revoked by the subsequent marriage.

(b) If you are under the age of 18, in Ontario you are known as a "minor," and generally are unable to make a valid will. Under the Succession Law Reform Act, a minor may make a valid will, notwithstanding the fact that he or she has not attained the age of 18 years, if the minor is married. As well, an individual under the age of 18 years may make a valid will if he or she is contemplating marriage and the will states that it is made in contemplation of the marriage to a specific, named person. In this case, the will would only take effect once the marriage to the named person took place.

(c) If you have a past history of mental disease or some lesser form of mental disorder such as a mental breakdown, you should consult a lawyer before making a will.

(d) If you are aged, you might also heed this warning in order to avoid any question of your mental capacity arising after your death. In order for a will to be valid in Ontario, the testator or testatrix must have a certain element of mental capacity, or, colloquially, "be of sound mind." The scope of this book does not permit a detailed legal discussion as to the necessary elements of mental competency. If there is any doubt whatsoever about your mental capacity or if you are aged, you should obtain legal counsel to ensure that the will is not attacked on the grounds of mental incapacity.

(e) If you are separated from your spouse, legal advice is essential. It is most important for you to have a will in order to avoid all or a portion of your assets from passing to your spouse. In addition, caution must be exercised in preparing a will which completely excludes your spouse. This warning may also be of significance to a divorced testator or testatrix. Part V of the Succession Law Reform Act substantially enlarges the group of individuals considered as dependants, and it may permit a spouse or a former spouse to attack the will and interfere with the disposition of the assets. The will may also be challenged by your spouse under the Family Law Act. Chapter 5 discusses these limitations on your ability to make a will.

(f) If your estate is likely to be large, you should certainly consult a lawyer if only in order to obtain advice on tax saving. Although there are no death duties in this province, the Income Tax Act (Canada) does impose a capital gains tax on death (see chapter 6). The capital gains tax which arises on death has, in essence, taken the place of the former Estate Tax Act (which imposed a federal death tax in the case of all deaths occurring before January 1, 1972) and the Succession Duty Act. Most large estates are complex in terms of types of assets held and where they are located. In this case, proper planning is a must and professional advice should be sought.

(g) If you own assets in a country other than Canada, you will have to comply not only with Ontario law, but also with the formal requirements for a will in the jurisdiction where the assets are located. You should, therefore, seek legal advice to ensure that your assets in a foreign country can be devised by your will.

(h) Always remember that a will is a technical document and a number of formalities must be followed in order to make it valid. Be very careful to follow the instructions set out in this book and if you have any questions or doubts about the validity of your will, have it reviewed by a lawyer.

d. LEGAL FEES

The drafting of a will is a "loss-leader" in the legal profession. In other words, a lawyer's charge for drafting a will is very reasonable. It is assumed that a person who consults a lawyer to draft a will very often employs the same lawyer for other legal services.

There is no consistency among lawyers with respect to the charges for the preparation of a will. A simple will involving no tax planning will usually cost between $100 and $300. Caution should, however, be exercised in relying upon these figures if there are complications involved in the estate or if a certain amount of tax planning is required. Never hesitate to ask a lawyer in advance for an estimated fee.

The lawyer in question may quote a set fee or, if the situation is more complicated, charge an hourly rate, ranging from $75 to $350 per hour. Though these sums may appear high, if large estates are involved or complex problems have to be faced, it will still be well worth the cost. These fees are for drawing up a will only. See chapter 3 for other legal fees that may be incurred when a lawyer becomes involved in the administration of the estate of a deceased person.

e. SHOULD EVERYONE HAVE A WILL?

The simple answer to this question is yes. A will is important for a variety of reasons. Should you die without a will (i.e., die "intestate"), the administration of your estate is complicated by the fact that you did not appoint an executor or executrix, and the court must be called upon to appoint someone to administer the estate.

More important, death without a will may result in your assets passing to heirs whom you did not wish to benefit from your death. Conversely, relatives and friends whom you would have wanted to benefit and whom you believed would inherit your estate may receive less than you intended or nothing at all.

The prime example of this is the common misconception that if a married man dies without leaving a will, all of his property passes to the surviving wife. This is not always the case and, where there are children of the marriage, the surviving wife may end up with less than one-half of her deceased husband's estate, and the children of the marriage with the remainder.

The value of having a will cannot be over-emphasized, regardless of the size of the estate involved. In order to simplify matters upon your death and in order to ensure that your property passes to those whom you wish to benefit, a will is essential.

f. THE COMMON-LAW SPOUSE

The common-law spouse is, as yet, given little recognition by our laws. Notwithstanding the recognition of illegitimate children by the Succession Law Reform Act, the legislation has done little to improve the situation of the common-law spouse. Part II of the act, which provides for the distribution of the estate of a person dying without a will, speaks only of a legal spouse. No provisions are made for the common-law spouse.

While a common-law spouse has a right under certain circumstances to claim as a dependant of the deceased common-law spouse (see chapter 5), it is vital for anyone living common-law to make a will providing specifically for his or her spouse. Should someone living common-law fail to make such a will, his or her property will be distributed on death as though the common-law spouse were a complete stranger. For the purposes of distributing the estate on an intestacy under Part II of the Succession Law Reform Act, the surviving common-law spouse will get *none* of the recognition of a legal spouse. The only rights of such common-law spouses arise as a consequence of their being able to establish their status as a dependant and make a claim against the estate of the deceased under Part V of the Succession Law Reform Act (see chapter 5).

g. RECOGNITION OF ILLEGITIMATE CHILDREN AND OTHER RELATIVES

The Succession Law Reform Act makes the rights of legitimate children and illegitimate children equal. Both are treated alike for the purposes of the distribution of the estate of a person dying without a will. This applies in both the case of a deceased mother and a deceased father. In fact, the legislation goes further. All illegitimate relatives are treated on an equal footing with legitimate ones. Under the act, if a person made a will leaving all of an estate "to my nephews," and there was an illegitimate nephew, he would share equally in the estate with the legitimate nephews.

The rules regarding legitimate and illegitimate heirs apply whether or not there is a will. In the case of a will, however, it is possible for a person to exclude the illegitimate relative by expressly stating this in the will. Specific words must be included in any will if illegitimate persons are to be denied benefits under that will. Thus, if you had four children of your marriage plus an illegitimate child from a relationship outside of the marriage, and you simply left your assets to be divided equally among your children, the division would be in five equal parts. The illegitimate child would share equally with the legitimate children. In order to avoid this, it is necessary for you to indicate in your will that you wish only your legitimate children to be considered when the distribution is made. Chapter 2 deals with this question again and contains an example of the type of clause that might be included in a will to exclude illegitimate beneficiaries.

It is anticipated that there may be some difficulty in establishing that a claimant is or is not the illegitimate child of the parent in question. The legislation casts an obligation on the executor or administrator to make reasonable enquiries in order to find people who may be entitled to a share of the estate as a result of a blood relationship arising from a birth outside of marriage. In the case of large families where benefits are being left to relatives more distant than children, these enquiries might be difficult to make.

h. WHAT HAPPENS IF YOU DIE WITHOUT A WILL?

Two gaps will exist in administering the estate of a person who dies intestate. First, no one will have been appointed by the deceased to act as an executor of the estate. Second, the deceased person will not have indicated in a legal form how he or she wishes the property to be distributed. Ontario law provides for each of these eventualities.

The Estates Act makes provision for the appointment of an "administrator" (or "administratrix," if female) to administer the estate of a person dying without a will. The functions of an administrator are basically the same as those of an executor (see chapter 4).

Men and women who look after the distribution of the assets of the estate either under a will or as a result of a court appointment may also be called personal representatives or estate trustees. Throughout this book, we will use the terms executor, administrator, personal representative, and estate trustee to apply to men and women alike.

Part II of the Succession Law Reform Act provides for the distribution of the property of a person dying without a will.

If you die without a will and leave no spouse or other blood relative, all of your property will pass to the provincial government. In these circumstances the property is said to escheat to the Crown.

2
DRAFTING YOUR OWN WILL

a. ESSENTIALS OF A WILL

You should exercise great care in preparing your own will. It is a very important document and if it is improperly prepared, it is not until after your death that an error is generally discovered. Then it is too late to rectify the error and your wishes may be frustrated by a distribution of the estate under the intestacy provisions of the Succession Law Reform Act (Part II) as though you had died without leaving any will. Sample #1 at the end of this chapter shows a basic will format.

As a general rule, a person must be 18 years of age or older to make a valid will in the province of Ontario. The exceptions to this rule were outlined in chapter 1.

If you intend to prepare your own will by using a pre-printed form or by starting from scratch, read through this chapter carefully before beginning. If you intend to make anything but the simplest of wills, consult a lawyer. The charge for preparing your will is small in comparison to the security you will have knowing that your will has been properly drafted and signed.

A will does not have to follow any special form. No legal words are needed. The will must clearly state your intentions. Lawyers usually follow set standard precedents (for examples, see Sample #1 and #2 at the end of this chapter), since over the years these precedents have proven most satisfactory. Wills forms can be purchased from most stationers in the province of Ontario (or see the coupon at the front of this book). Your will need not be typewritten, but may be in your handwriting or that of any other person, as long as it is properly executed.

A will generally starts out by identifying the testator (you) and stating your place of residence and occupation. This is usually done by words such as the following: "This is the last will and testament of me, John Doe, presently residing at 111 Principle Street in the City of Toronto in the Municipality of Metropolitan Toronto, Laborer."

The first clause of the will should state that all previous wills are revoked. If you make more than one will during your lifetime, the will bearing the latest date governs. It is, however, always advisable to expressly revoke earlier wills in order to avoid any confusion or question at the time of death. It is customary to insert the following clause as the first clause in any will: "I hereby revoke all wills, codicils, and testamentary dispositions of every nature and kind whatsoever previously made by me."

The Succession Law Reform Act recognizes the validity of a holograph will. This is a will wholly in your handwriting and signed by yourself. A holograph will needs no witnesses. A wills form with some of the clauses preprinted would not qualify as a holograph will since the statute provides that it must be wholly in the deceased's handwriting. Otherwise, two witnesses to the signature of the person making the will are required. In the case of either the traditional form of will or the holograph will, your signature should come on the last page of the will after all the provisions which you wish to make have been set forth. When signing the traditional form of will, you and the two witnesses should all be present at the same time, the two witnesses watching you sign the will and watching each other sign in the spaces provided. If these rules are strictly followed, the will cannot be attacked on account of improper execution.

A very important limitation on who is able to be a witness to a will should be noted at this point. Any person who is to receive any benefit under the will, i.e., any beneficiary, should not be a witness to the will. Likewise, neither the husband nor the wife of any beneficiary under the will should be a witness. If this rule is broken, the will is not invalidated, but the gift to the beneficiary who acted as a witness or to the beneficiary whose spouse acted as a witness will not be effective. The will will be read as though no such gift were contained in it and the part of the estate which would have gone to such beneficiary would pass to the residuary beneficiary, i.e., the person to whom the remainder or the residue of the estate is left.

The Succession Law Reform Act allows for the court to give relief from the effect of this rule of law, provided that it is satisfied neither the witness nor the spouse exercised any improper, undue influence on the person making the will. For the gift to be effective, the beneficiary would bear the onus of proving lack of undue influence to the court. Rather than take the risks inherent in making such a court application necessary, it would be wiser to ensure that neither of the two witnesses is a beneficiary or the spouse of a beneficiary under the will. No such problem with witnesses arises, of course, if the will qualifies as a holograph will, as witnesses are not required.

If the will is contained on more than one page of paper, it is a good idea for you and the two witnesses (if you are not making a holograph will) to place your respective initials in the lower right-hand corner of each of the pages of the will, with the exception of the final page, upon which the signatures appear. This is not a legal requirement but has the effect of preventing any person at a later date from substituting some of the earlier pages for those which were present at the time the document was signed. Such substitution of pages could be readily carried out if the pages preceding the signing page were not initialed.

If the will contains any noticeable corrections, insertions, or deletions, these should be initialed by you and the two witnesses, if any, at the time the will is signed. If this rule is not followed, when the will is submitted to the court after your death, it will be necessary for your executor to convince the judge at a special hearing that the will was not tampered with after you signed it in front of the witnesses. Your executor will have to show that the changes were made by you before the will was signed. A safer procedure is to retype or rewrite any page, with the required corrections, before the will is signed.

After the will is signed and witnessed, it is a good idea to complete an Affidavit of Execution. This is a sworn statement signed by one of the witnesses that identifies the will and confirms that both witnesses were present to see it signed. This affidavit will be required when the will is submitted for probate. At that time, the witnesses may not be readily available or may have died. It is therefore wise to complete the affidavit immediately after the will is signed.

The Affidavit of Execution must be signed by the witness in the presence of a notary public or a commissioner of oaths. A sample affidavit is shown in Sample #9.

b. HOW TO APPOINT A PERSONAL REPRESENTATIVE

No one under the age of 18 can serve as your personal representative (formerly known as executor). It is always advisable to select someone who is of the same age as you or younger. Do not appoint someone who is 20 years older than you to be your personal representative, as he or she will probably die before you and the appointment will be ineffective.

Likewise it is pointless to name someone as a personal representative without first checking to see if he or she would be willing to take on the responsibility. There is no compulsion on anyone named as a personal representative to serve. A refusal like this is technically known as "renunciation." If the proposed person, for example, tells you that he or she would rather not be made responsible for the job, you would be very wise to appoint someone else.

If you wish, you may appoint more than one person to act as your personal representative, especially if your estate is large. Many wills also provide for an alternative personal representative. For example, if you appoint a personal representative to look after your estate, you may provide that, if this first person should die, or be unable to act for any reason, the second named personal representative is to assume the duties of administering the estate.

There are no magic words required to appoint a personal representative in a will; any words that clearly indicate that the person named by you is to carry out the will's provisions will have the effect of constituting the named person as a personal representative. Your will should simply be as clear as possible, since you will not be available to provide an explanation when a question arises. The following is an example of a clause which would be inserted to appoint a personal representative:

> I nominate and appoint my wife, Mary Doe, to be the personal representative of this, my will.

If an alternative personal representative is desired, the following words should be added to the above appointment:

> In the event that my said wife shall predecease me or refuse or be unable to act or to continue to act as personal representative of this, my will, I nominate and appoint my solicitor, Gordon Goodbody, to be the personal representative of this, my will, in the place and stead of my said wife.

c. COMMON DISASTER CLAUSE

Most wills drawn by lawyers include a common disaster provision. An example of such a provision is the underlined portion of the following clause:

I give all my property of every nature and kind to my wife, Mary Doe, <u>provided that she survives me for a period of 30 days.</u>

Under Ontario law, when two people die at the same time or in circumstances where it is uncertain who died first, the property of each person is to be disposed of as if the person owning the property had survived the other. An example would be the case of John and Mary Doe. They each made a will in which all the assets of the one were left to the surviving spouse; the wills contained no common disaster clause or alternative gift provisions. They had no children and were both killed instantly in a car accident. For the purpose of the wife's will she would be presumed to survive her husband, while for the husband's will, he would be presumed to survive his wife.

Thus, a common disaster clause is not necessary to make provision for the situation where it is unclear who died first, but it is still a good idea to include one. Assume that a wife survives her husband by 20 minutes. Without a common disaster clause all of the husband's estate would pass to the wife because she had actually survived him. This would involve administering the assets of the husband as part of two separate and distinct estates, with the attendant duplication of cost and effort. Furthermore, all of the assets would end up going to those named as the alternative beneficiaries of the wife's will, if any, or passing to the wife's blood relatives as though she had died without a will.

It should be obvious, then, that a will should always contain a "common disaster clause" where the beneficiary and the person making the will stand a chance of dying in a common disaster. This is obviously the case with husband and wife who frequently travel together. Joint disaster need not be a consideration if the testator and the beneficiary are rarely or never together since a common disaster could not occur.

It should be pointed out that there is nothing magic about the 30-day period commonly used by lawyers. Any period may be chosen. It is generally thought, however, that 30 days is neither too long nor too short a period to serve the purpose for which it is intended.

d. ALTERNATIVE GIFT PROVISION

The common disaster clause described above is usually combined with a gift of the estate to an alternative beneficiary or beneficiaries, who will inherit the estate if the original beneficiary dies before or within 30 days of the testator. This provision ensures that the estate will pass to the intended beneficiaries. If there is no such provision, and the original beneficiary dies, the estate will be divided in accordance with the rules of intestate succession used when there is no will (see chapter 4, section c.). The following is an example of an alternative gift provision:

> In the event that my wife, Mary Doe, predeceases me or dies within 30 days of the date of my death, then the gift to my wife Mary Doe shall be void and I GIVE, DEVISE, AND BEQUEATH all my property of every nature and kind to my daughter, Denise Doe, for her own use absolutely.

e. SPECIFIC BEQUESTS

A person making a will may want to leave specific items or a fixed amount of money to a relative, friend, or charity. A gift of money should be made in the following fashion:

> I give to my niece, Jenny Doe, the sum of ONE THOUSAND DOLLARS ($1 000).

If a specific article is to be left to a named person, then the article in question should be described in sufficient detail in the will so that the personal representative will be able to identify the item. For instance, in the event that John Doe, the testator, wishes to leave to his niece, Jenny, a painting, words to the following effect should be inserted in the will:

> I give to my niece, Jenny Doe, my painting titled 'Autumn Leaves' by Tom Thompson.

This detail would probably be sufficient to identify the painting the testator had in mind.

After providing for the revocation of former wills and appointing a personal representative, it is advisable to provide for any specific bequests of the sort outlined above. Quite often a person making a will provides for a few specific bequests of money or specific items and then goes on to provide that the remainder or the residue of the estate be delivered over to another named person. Alternatively, the residue may be divided among a group of people, identified either by name or by description (such as "my children").

An example of a gift of the remainder of the residue of an estate is as follows:

> I direct my personal representative to pay or transfer all the rest and residue of my estate to my sister, Sue Doe, provided that she survives me for a period of 30 days.

An example of a gift of the residue to a group might be as follows:

> I direct my personal representative to divide the rest and residue of my estate into as many equal shares as there shall be children of mine alive at the time of my death and to pay or transfer one of such equal shares to each of such children.

All wills should contain a clause disposing of the residue of the estate. Some people will provide an extensive list of specific requests disposing of all the assets to various relatives and friends by specifically naming the asset to be left to the beneficiary in question. They then feel it is unnecessary to provide for a residuary gift in the will. This is a mistake since one or more of the named beneficiaries may die before the testator dies. In this situation, the gift to the beneficiary would not be effective and the will would not provide what was to happen to the asset in question. A residuary gift would prevent this from happening: the gift to the deceased beneficiary would fall into the residue of the estate and pass in accordance with the clause disposing of the residue of the estate.

A residuary gift is also important since, after making a will, a testator may acquire new and different assets. Even if he or she may be old and feel that there is little chance of acquiring any other assets of any consequence, this belief has often been proven wrong; to protect against such newly acquired assets not being dealt with by the will, a residuary clause should always be used.

f. SPECIAL CLAUSES

You may include in your will an almost infinite variety of special clauses beyond the normal provisions which we have discussed above. This section of the chapter will deal with some of these clauses.

1. Life estate

Where you have accumulated a fairly large estate, you may provide for what is known as a "life estate" or a "life interest." By doing this, you are able to control an asset like land or money after your death.

The most common clause of this sort permits the spouse to make use of the matrimonial home during the remainder of his or her lifetime and provides that upon his or her death the home will be given outright to the child of the deceased.

Another possibility is to leave to your spouse a life interest in a sum of money. If a will provides for the spouse to receive a life interest in $100 000, the $100 000 is invested and the spouse receives only the interest on the $100 000 for the balance of his or her lifetime. Once the spouse dies, he or she has no further interest in the money set aside and it passes to another beneficiary as provided in the will. The purpose of these provisions is to prevent assets from being squandered, or to provide a means of support for someone who is not capable of managing the asset.

The following is an example of a clause creating a life interest.

> Provided that my wife, Mary Doe, survives me for a period of 30 days, I direct my personal representative to permit her to use and occupy the marital home located at 111 Principle Street, Toronto, for the balance of her lifetime or as long as she does not remarry. Upon the death of my said wife or in the event of her remarriage, I direct my personal representative to deliver my said home to my son, David Doe, for his own use absolutely.

Exercise caution in creating life interests in a home-drawn will as there are problems with making such gifts enforceable and ensuring the greatest amount of tax relief for the beneficiaries. Legal advice should be sought.

2. Gifts to minors

No one can pay out a gift or share of the estate to a beneficiary who is under 18. If a gift is made to an underage beneficiary, the personal representative must hold the gift until the beneficiary reaches 18.

Your personal representative's duty is to protect the gift to the beneficiary and to invest it to produce a reasonable but safe income during the period in which the money is held. Frequently, the personal representative is permitted to "encroach" upon the capital of an infant's gift if, in his or her discretion, the capital is needed to maintain the child. For such a right of encroachment to exist, it must be given in the will.

Thus, the personal representative has the power to pay out certain amounts of the gift to the infant, or to use certain amounts for the infant's benefit. As the word "benefit" has been interpreted very widely by the courts, a clause permitting a personal representative, for example, to encroach upon a gift of money for the infant's benefit, permits him or her to pay the money out for practically any worthwhile cause.

While it is not possible for a minor to receive his or her share of an estate until attaining the age of 18, it is possible to provide for a beneficiary's share to be held longer by an appropriate clause in the will. For example, it is still quite common for wills to provide for children's shares in an estate to be held until such children reach the age of 21. Sample #3 at the end of this chapter provides for the children's shares to be paid over to them when they reach 18. It would be quite possible, however, to substitute 21 for 18 in Sample #3, in which case the shares of the children would be held and invested by the personal representative until they reached the age of 21.

It should be noted, however, that if all of the beneficiaries of the estate are over the age of 18, and there are no conditions attached to the gift except for the passage of time until they reach the age of 21 (or other age stated in the will), the court may order the executor to pay over the moneys to the beneficiaries even though they have not attained the age stated in the will.

3. Investments

Ontario law limits the kinds of investments a personal representative can make with the assets of an estate.

In the normal situation, the estate of a deceased person is distributed to the various beneficiaries named in the will immediately after the death of that person. Most wills provide for this immediate distribution of assets. However, it is impossible to wind up the estate in situations where a life interest is provided or where there are infants involved. The personal representative must hold the gift and invest the funds until the life interest expires, or the infant reaches 18 or such later age as the will provides. The gift must be invested; it cannot be hidden in a mattress and then paid out when the time comes.

The personal representative is required to make only those investments that are quite "safe," with the result that the return for the investment may be lower than would be realized from other available investments. The Trustee Act (Ontario) sets out the rather limited range of investments normally open to a personal representative. If you wish to give your personal representative more freedom, you may do so by inserting a specific clause in the will allowing the personal representative to invest at his or her own discretion. You might use a clause like the following:

> Notwithstanding the provisions of the Trustee Act and any other law pertaining to the form of investments in which trustees are authorized to invest trust funds, I hereby authorize my personal representative to invest any portion of my estate in such investments as she may see fit.

4. Exclusion of illegitimate children

Since the Succession Law Reform Act makes the rights of legitimate and illegitimate children and other heirs equal as beneficiaries if they are referred to as a class, i.e., "my children" or "my nieces" or "the children of my neighbor, Mary Brown," a person making a will must expressly exclude any illegitimate beneficiaries if he or she does not wish them to inherit. The following is an example of a clause that would have this effect:

> Any reference in my will or any codicil hereto to a person in terms of a relationship to another person determined by blood or marriage, shall not include a person born outside of marriage or a person who comes within the description traced through another person who was born outside of marriage, provided that any person who has been legally adopted shall be regarded as having been born in lawful wedlock to his or her adopting parent.

5. Taxes and debts

Although by law the personal representative is obliged to pay all taxes and debts of the deceased before distributing assets of the estate to the named beneficiaries, it is common to find a clause to this effect in wills today. The following is an example of a type of clause commonly inserted in wills:

> I direct my personal representative to pay out of my estate my just debts, funeral and testamentary expenses, and all income taxes or taxes payable in connection with and arising out of my death.

6. Majority rule

In larger estates, two or three people are often appointed personal representatives of the estate. The rule with regard to multiple personal representatives is that all actions must be unanimously approved. If you do not wish this rule to apply to your personal representatives, and prefer that the majority rule govern, use a clause like the following:

> I hereby direct that the decision of a majority of my personal representatives shall be decisive upon any matter and the decision of the majority shall be binding upon all personal representatives and beneficiaries.

7. Death of a personal representative

Where you appoint more than one personal representative to act at the same time, you may provide that if one dies the surviving personal representative shall appoint a replacement. If this is your wish, a clause to this effect inserted in your will is effective. If no provision like this is made, a surviving personal representative has full power to continue on with the administration of the estate regardless of the death of the other person.

8. Custody of children

A fairly common provision in the will of a person with young children is the appointment of someone to have custody of the children if both parents die. A related provision allows parents to appoint a guardian of their children's property. A clause such as the following might be used:

> In the event that my spouse predeceases me, and any child of mine is under the age of 18 years at my death, I appoint my sister, Sally Doe, to have custody of such child, and to be the guardian of such child's property, during his or her respective minority.

Of course, the guardian's approval should be obtained before the appointment. Furthermore, be sure that he or she is of an age suitable to raise infant children. You would not want to make an 80-year-old person responsible for a 12-year-old child.

Under Ontario law, the appointment of a custodian and guardian of your child's property is valid for up to 90 days. In order to make the appointment permanent, the person named in your will as custodian or guardian must apply to court within 90 days from the date of death. Generally speaking, the courts will uphold the wishes of the parent, and will approve the application for permanent custody or guardianship. However, if the court believes the child is better off with someone else, the appointment made in the will can be disregarded.

9. Funeral instructions

More and more people are concerned today about the manner in which they are to be buried or the cost of such burial. You may include in your will instructions to your personal representative about the means or cost of the burial of your body. The will may, therefore, contain a clause stating that you wish to be cremated and that your ashes should be disposed of in a certain fashion. Alternatively, you may provide for burial in a particular location or through a certain funeral home.

A fairly common clause is a direction to keep the expenses of the funeral to a bare minimum. If this is your wish, then a simple statement in your will to this effect will oblige the personal representative to abide by your wishes. It should be borne in mind that where the spouse of the deceased is not the personal representative, it is the duty and right of the personal representative, rather than the surviving spouse, to arrange for the funeral of the deceased. The personal representative is entitled to spend only a reasonable amount for the burial. The beneficiaries may sue a personal representative for any "excess expenses" arising from extravagance or disregard for the instructions regarding burial contained in the will.

10. Body donation

People often direct that their bodies are to be delivered to a local university or medical school for research purposes. Once the body has served its purpose, the medical school arranges for the disposition of the body at no cost to the estate of the deceased. It is generally necessary for everyone who wishes to donate his or her body to research to contact the particular school involved and complete a "donor card." For example, the Department of Anatomy of the University of Toronto requests that a person wishing to donate his or her body register with them before death. In fact, the university has published a booklet setting out its requirements. A copy can be obtained by calling (416) 978-2692.

11. Organ transplants

Occasionally a person will wish to make certain organs of his or her body available for transplant purposes. A clause such as the following might be inserted in the will:

> It is my desire and I so instruct my personal representative to make any of my physical organs available for the purpose of transplant or research but I expressly forbid the use of my body, as a whole, for purposes of medical research.

The second part can, of course, be omitted if you do not object to the use of your body for medical research.

12. Eye bank

It is now fairly common for people to bequeath their eyes to the Eye Bank run by the Canadian National Institute for the Blind. Such a gift should be worded in the following fashion:

> Should my eyes be considered useful by the Eye Bank of Canada, I direct my personal respresentative to carry out the arrangements that I have made so that my eyes will be left to the Eye Bank of Canada under the auspices of the C.N.I.B.

Arrangements for gifts like this must be made during the lifetime of the donor. Donor cards may be obtained from the

Canadian National Institute for the Blind by calling (416) 480-7465. They should be completed and a portion returned to the Institute. You should carry with you your portion of the donor card as it serves to notify anyone that, in the event of your death, your eyes have been bequeathed to the Eye Bank of Canada and that immediate steps should be taken to ensure that your wishes are carried out. To be useful for transplant purposes, eyes must be removed within 12 to 16 hours of death. Age appears to be no barrier to the usefulness of eyes for transplant purposes, although if death has resulted from certain causes, such as cancer, the eyes may not be acceptable for transplant purposes.

In any case where the will contains directions for burial, or for the disposition of the body to medical science, or bequeaths organs or eyes, the personal representative named in the will must be advised of these provisions immediately after the will is signed. If these provisions come as a surprise after the testator has died, it may be too late to put them into effect, since the will is often not consulted until two or three days after the death. Common sense should be exercised in such circumstances and steps taken to ensure that wishes of this nature are carried out.

13. Charity

You may wish to leave money to your favorite charity. Such a gift should be explicitly set out in the will. A charity is defined as any institution established for charitable purposes including —

(a) relief of poverty,

(b) advancement of education,

(c) advancement of religion, and

(d) other purposes beneficial to the community.

A charitable donation could be worded as follows:

> I bequeath the sum of $10 000 to the governing body of Westgate High School at Kitchener for the purpose of acquiring equipment and facilities for the playing of all sports.

Be sure to identify the charity correctly. You may wish to contact them and find out their proper legal name.

14. R.R.S.P.

Special consideration should be given to a Registered Retirement Savings Plan, if you have one. A clause such as this may be inserted in the will:

> I DIRECT THAT my personal representative shall pay and transfer to my husband all amounts which may be payable to my estate by the Northeastern Insurance Company, trustees of my Registered Retirement Savings Plan established by me during my lifetime, if he survives me for a period of 30 days, provided that if he shall predecease me or die within a period of 30 days after my death, I hereby designate my son, Gordon Doe, to be the beneficiary of the proceeds.

15. Accounts receivable

If your estate is likely to include many accounts receivable, considerable tax savings can be obtained by leaving such accounts to a designated beneficiary. If the will does not specifically provide for a bequest of accounts receivable, they will be included in the income for the year of death at their face value less a reserve for bad debts.

If, however, a specific bequest is made in the will of the receivables, then they are non-taxable in the hands of the beneficiary until the time when the beneficiary either disposes of them at a discount price or collects the receivables over a period of time. You might use the following clause to accomplish this:

> I DIRECT THAT my personal representative shall pay and transfer to my wife for her own use absolutely all of my accounts receivable if she shall survive me for a period of 30 days, provided that, if she shall predecease

me or should survive me but die within the period of 30 days after my death, I hereby designate my son, Gordon Doe, as recipient.

16. Separate property clause

Under the Family Law Act, married persons who separate or divorce must share equally most of the property that they acquire during their marriage. One of the exceptions to this rule is property inherited by a spouse from a third party. However, the income from inherited property is not exempt from claims to equalize net family property unless the testator specifically states in his or her will that it is to be excluded.

For example, a testator who owns a cottage property may make a will leaving the property to his daughter. On the death of the testator, the daughter receives the property and rents it out to tenants. The daughter later separates from her husband and must equalize her net family property with that of her spouse. The inherited cottage will be exempt from division, but the income from the property will have to be divided unless the appropriate clause preventing this is inserted in the will. The following is an example of a clause commonly used for this purpose:

> Any benefit, whether as to income or capital or both, or income from capital, to which any person shall become entitled in accordance with the provisions of this my will or any codicil thereto, shall not fall into any community of property which may exist between any such person and his or her spouse and shall not form part of his or her net family property for any purpose or purposes of the Family Law Act, 1986, in the province of Ontario and any amendments thereto or any successor legislation thereto, but shall only be paid by my trustees to such person on the condition that the same shall remain the separate property of such person, free from the control of his or her spouse. The separate receipt of such person shall be a discharge to my trustees in respect of any such payment.

17. Power of sale clause

The personal representative of the estate is often required to sell some of the assets of the estate in order to pay debts of the estate or to divide the value of the assets among the beneficiaries. Since the assets of the estate belong to the beneficiaries, the personal representative requires some type of authority from the testator to sell the assets and convert the estate into liquid form. The following is an example of a clause in the will that accomplishes this purpose:

> I AUTHORIZE AND EMPOWER my personal representative and trustees, in their absolute discretion, to sell, mortgage, and convey all or any part of my real estate or personal estate for cash or for credit or partly for cash and partly for credit at such times, for such amounts, and on such terms as my personal representative and trustees may deem advisable.

g. WHAT ABOUT DEBTS?

A will usually provides that the personal representative shall pay all the debts of the deceased outstanding at the time of death. Such a provision is not essential since it is the legal obligation of all personal representatives to pay the debts of the estate before distributing anything to beneficiaries. No specific direction in the will is needed to carry this out. In addition, a personal representative is obliged to pay all fees in connection with probating the will, all funeral expenses, and all legal fees before paying out bequests under the will. In the event that there are insufficient assets of the estate to pay all these items, the law provides for priorities of payment.

There may be sufficient assets of the estate to cover all the debts and expenses outlined above, but the assets may be insufficient to pay all the specific bequests and gifts of money. In this event, the assets that remain after payment of debts will be divided among the beneficiaries proportionately according to the amounts they would have received had the assets been sufficient. Of course, in this situation the residuary beneficiary would not receive anything because there would be no residue.

h. HOW TO MAKE CHANGES IN YOUR WILL (CODICILS)

The situation often arises where a person makes a will and, subsequently, circumstances change so that he or she wishes to make minor alterations in the will. Instead of making a completely new will, it is possible to simply make a "codicil." A codicil is an amendment to the will, stating that certain provisions of the will are now to be revoked and possibly substituting new provisions for the revoked provisions. A codicil is commonly used when a beneficiary or the person named as personal representative dies during the lifetime of the testator or testatrix. In these situations, the will should be revised to reflect the changed circumstances.

A codicil, like a will, is a testamentary document and all the rules outlined earlier in this chapter about the execution and validity of a will apply to a codicil. If wholly in the handwriting of the person making the codicil, the codicil does not require any witnesses, as it is held to be the equivalent of a holograph will. Otherwise, as in the case of a traditional form of will, a codicil requires two witnesses to the signature of the person making the will. These witnesses need not be the original witnesses to the will.

A codicil should start with the words:

> This is a codicil to the last will of me, Jane Doe, of the City of Toronto, in the Province of Ontario, which said last will bears the date of the 7th day of January, 19—.

It is important to tie together the original will and the codicil that amends it by referring to the date of the will in the opening words of the codicil. The codicil should then go on to state which clauses are revoked or amended and, if a new provision is being substituted for one which has been revoked, should set forth such new provision. As a general rule, the final clause of the codicil should always state that you confirm the will in all other respects.

The effect of making a codicil is that the will and the codicil are read together and any amendments contained in the codicil are read into the will as though they had appeared there in the first place. A series of codicils may be made and in each instance the changes in each codicil will be read into the original will. If too many changes are made, a new will should be prepared incorporating all of the changes to date. Sample #4 following this chapter is an example of a codicil.

It is not advisable to amend the provisions of a will by making physical changes or writing on the will. It is possible to do this if proper procedure is followed, but it is strongly recommended that changes be carried out by using a codicil or making a new will.

i. HOW OFTEN SHOULD YOUR WILL BE REVISED?

Once a will has been made, it should be reviewed at least every five years, and more frequently if there is a death among the beneficiaries. There is no law requiring that a will be revised from time to time and, should you die leaving a will 50 years old, the will is perfectly valid and will be effective to pass on the assets of the estate. The reason for reviewing and revising your will is a practical one rather than a legal one.

Over the years, friendships change, relatives die, and the value of your estate may change considerably. In larger estates, changes in tax laws may prompt a change in the will in order to minimize income taxes and death duties. For all these reasons your will should be reviewed on a regular basis and, if it no longer makes appropriate provisions for the existing situation, it should be revised.

Minor amendments can be made by way of a simple codicil. If the changes are major, a new will should be drawn up. The new will should expressly revoke the earlier will.

Many solicitors recommend that when a new will is signed, the old will be physically destroyed. This may have its disadvantages if, for some reason, the later will proves invalid. In such circumstances the former will might be revived and ruled valid by a court. It may therefore be advisable in some cases to retain both the old and new wills together.

j. HOW TO REVOKE YOUR WILL

As previously mentioned, a will is revoked by the making of a new will which is either inconsistent with the former will or which expressly revokes the former will. The most recent will always governs.

You can also revoke your will by physically destroying it. Should you then die without having made a new will, the estate will be distributed as though the will that was destroyed had never existed.

If you wish to revoke an existing will, but it is impractical or impossible for you to destroy it, for example, if the will is in your safety deposit box at the bank, you may make a codicil revoking the will. You simply state that your last will and testament is revoked in all respects, and you identify the will being revoked by referring to the date on which it was signed. A codicil of this sort might read as follows:

> This is the second codicil to the last will of me, Tony Testator, which last will bears the date of the 25th day of July, 19—.
>
> 1. I revoke in all respects my last will and testament which bears the date of the 25th day of July, 19—.
>
> 2. I further revoke in all respects the first codicil to my said will, which codicil bears the date of the 16th day of September, 19—.
>
> In witness whereof I, Tony Testator, have to this second codicil to my last will contained on this single sheet of paper subscribed my name at the City of Lights in the Province of Ontario, on this 30th day of April, 19—.

SIGNED, PUBLISHED, AND DECLARED
by the said Tony Testator, the above named
testator, as and for the second codicil to his last
will and testament, in the presence of us, who   _Tony Testator_
in his presence, at his request and in the presence
of each other have hereunto subscribed our
names as witnesses attesting same.

I. B. Witness   _U. B. Witness_
Witness   Witness

107 Probate Row   _105 Probate Row_
Address   Address

Clerk   _Saleswoman_
Occupation   Occupation

The codicil must then be signed like any other codicil, i.e.,
in the presence of two witnesses, unless it is wholly in your
handwriting, in which case only your signature is required.
Once signed, it effectively revokes the earlier will.

k. MARRIAGE AND WILLS

The Succession Law Reform Act says a will is automatically
revoked by marriage except in certain narrow circumstances.
Upon marrying, you should make a new will as soon as
possible.

A will is not revoked by marriage when the will was
made prior to marriage and in contemplation of the specific
marriage. The will should state on its face that it is being
prepared in contemplation of your marriage to a certain
named person. If it does so, the will will not be revoked by
subsequent marriage to that person.

A will made before a marriage also remains valid if,
within one year after the death, the surviving spouse elects
to take the share provided for him or her under that will. For

31

example, John and Mary had been living together for several years and John had made a will leaving all of his estate to Mary. They then decided to get married and had several children, but John did not make a new will. When John died, Mary could elect to accept the share bequeathed to her under that early will (100% of the estate) instead of accepting the portion that would come to her if John's will were invalid and the estate were divided according to the law (she would receive less than 100% of the estate).

l. DIVORCE AND WILLS

The Succession Law Reform Act states that unless a contrary intention appears in the will itself, any gifts or bequests to a former spouse and any appointment of a former spouse as a personal representative are automatically revoked by a judgment granting a divorce to the spouses. The will remains perfectly valid (it is not wholly revoked), but it is read as though the former spouse predeceased the person making the will. For the purposes of the administration of an estate in accordance with the provisions of the act, the divorced spouse is treated as if he or she were dead.

m. IF UNABLE TO READ AND WRITE

A will may be made by a person who is unable to read and write. In such a case, the verbal instructions of the testator are transcribed onto paper. Prior to the signing of the will, it should be read over in full, word for word, to the testator. The will should then be signed by the testator making a mark, which usually takes the form of an X, on the will. One of the witnesses should then indicate beside the X that it is the mark of the testator. The witnesses then proceed to sign the will as in the normal case. However, the declaration of the witnesses which appears above their names is amended to confirm the will was read over to the testator and he or she appeared to understand it. A sample declaration of this kind appears as follows:

> Signed by the testatrix, Jane Doe, as her last will, after the same had first been read over to the testatrix in our presence and it appeared to be perfectly understood and approved by her, in the presence of us, both present at the same time, who at her request, in her presence, and in the presence of each other, have hereunto subscribed our names as witnesses.

Needless to say, it would be impossible for such a person to make a holograph will.

n. THE "LIVING WILL"

Advances in medical science have enabled doctors to keep someone "alive" when, in fact, the person may be totally reliant on extraordinary, artificial means of life support.

A "living will" is, in essence, a declaration stating your wishes about whether and how you want your life to be extended through the use of medical machines. This "living will" is a separate document from your will, and in reality, it is not a will at all.

In 1996, the government of Ontario passed a new statute known as The Health Care Consent Act. This legislation gives legal effect to a living will. It allows a person to express wishes with respect to treatment, which will remain valid if that person later becomes mentally incapable. These wishes may be expressed in a Power of Attorney for Personal Care, another written form, or even orally.

Common sense would dictate that a person's wishes regarding medical treatment should be put in writing, so that there is no disagreement or confusion when the time comes to give or refuse Consent to Treatment.

A sample living will or power of attorney for personal care might include the following declaration:

> Death is as much a reality as birth, growth, maturity, and old age — it is the one certainty of life. If the time comes when I, Tony Testator, can no longer take part in decisions for my own future, let this statement stand as an expression of my wishes, while I am still of sound mind.

If the situation should arise in which I am suffering from a terminal condition and I am no longer mentally competent, I request that I be allowed to die and not be kept alive by artificial means or by the use of life-sustaining procedures. I do not fear death itself as much as the indignities of deterioration, dependence, and hopeless pain. I ask, therefore, that medication be mercifully administered to me to alleviate suffering even though this may hasten the moment of death.

This request is made after careful consideration. I hope you who care for me will feel morally bound to follow its mandate. I recognize that this appears to place heavy responsibility upon you, but it is with the intention of relieving you of such responsibility and of placing it upon myself in accordance with my strong convictions, that this statement is made.

Two blank living wills forms are included in *Have You Made Your Will?*, the will and estate planning kit available from the publisher.

o. SUMMARY OF STEPS IN MAKING YOUR WILL

If you wish to make your own will, the following points should act as a summary of various matters you should bear in mind.

(a) Write down on a piece of paper your debts and your assets. Make a list of those people you wish to benefit under your will. Prepare a brief statement showing who your beneficiaries are to be and precisely what they are to receive.

(b) You are now in a position to start to draft your will. You may either type your own or use a will form available from the publisher and adapt it according to the instructions included in this book and the examples shown at the end of this chapter. Be sure that your handwriting is clear. The will should be typed, if at all possible. If not, print.

(c) Consult in advance the person or persons whom you propose to name as personal representative so that you can be sure they are prepared to assume the duty in the event of your death. It is pointless to execute a will naming someone as a personal representative when you know that he or she is not prepared to assume the responsibility. Take similar precautions with your proposed alternative personal respresentative. Remember, everyone should name an alternative, if at all possible.

(d) After you have written or typed your will in which you dispose of all your assets and appoint a personal representative, sign the document. Needless to say, if you do not sign your will it will have no significance whatever at the time of your death. Even though the document has been drawn up by you, it must be properly signed by you and your witnesses (unless a holograph will) prior to your death. Unless the will is a holograph will, two witnesses are required and, remember, they should not be beneficiaries under the will or the spouses of beneficiaries.

(e) If the will is not a holograph will, you and the two witnesses get together in the same room. You should, in the presence of the two witnesses and with the two witnesses watching you, sign at the end of the will. The two witnesses should then each sign. If the will is longer than one page, you and the two witnesses should initial each page of the will with the exception of the page upon which the signatures already appear. This renders more difficult the fraudulent substitution of pages after the will has been properly signed.

(f) At the end of the will, insert the date on which it was signed. This is essential, especially in cases where you have made more than one will. If one of the wills is undated, it becomes impossible to tell which will governs the disposition of your estate. No will should be signed without the day, month, and year being stated clearly.

(g) You should sign only one copy of the will. Several copies of the will might be typed or written and it is always a good idea to deliver an unsigned copy of the will to your personal representative. This allows him or her to become familiar with its provisions and, upon your death, to have immediate access to a copy of the will.

The original signed will should be kept in a safe place, like a safety deposit box. If you do not have a safety deposit box and do not wish to bear the annual expense of obtaining one simply to store your will, an alternative is available. You may take your original will to the local registrar of the court for the county or region in which you reside. The registrar is obliged to accept the will for safekeeping and will store the executed will indefinitely for a nominal charge. If you ever wish to retrieve your will, you may do so by simply returning to the office of the registrar of the court and establishing your identity.

As a general rule, a solicitor who prepares a will for a client will store the original in his or her vault should the client request this service. No charge is usually made for such safekeeping. This may save the cost of a safety deposit box if you choose to have your will prepared by a lawyer.

SAMPLE #1
BASIC WILL

Sample will for use by a married man or married woman (with children 18 years of age or over), leaving everything to the spouse if the spouse survives for a period of 30 days, with alternate bequests in the event that the spouse does not survive. This form may be readily adapted for use by a married man or woman without children or by an unmarried person.

THIS IS THE LAST WILL AND TESTAMENT of me, JOHN DAVID COOPER, of the City of Mississauga in the Regional Municipality of Peel in the Province of Ontario, Engineer.

I.   I HEREBY REVOKE all wills, codicils, and testamentary dispositions of every nature and kind whatsoever by me heretofore made.

II.   I NOMINATE, CONSTITUTE, AND APPOINT my wife, LORRAINE ELIZABETH COOPER, to be the sole personal representative of this, my will; provided that should my said wife predecease me, or should she be unwilling or unable to act, then I NOMINATE, CONSTITUTE, AND APPOINT my daughter, ANDREA JANE SMITHERS, to be the personal representative of this, my will, in the place and stead of my said wife.

III.   I DIRECT my personal representative to pay my just debts, funeral, and testamentary expenses and all income taxes, estate, inheritance and succession duties, or taxes wheresoever payable.

IV.   I GIVE, DEVISE AND BEQUEATH all of my property of every nature and kind and wheresoever situate, including any property over which I may have a general power of appointment, to my personal representative on the following trusts:

(a)   In the event that my said wife, LORRAINE ELIZABETH COOPER, survives me for a period of thirty days, I direct my executrix to pay or transfer to my said wife the residue of my estate for her own use absolutely;

(b)   In the event that my said wife shall predecease me or, surviving me, die within a period of thirty days following my decease, I direct my personal representative to divide the residue of my estate equally among my three children, JOHN JAMES COOPER, LISA ANN COOPER, AND ANDREA JANE SMITHERS, for their own use absolutely; provided that if any of my said children shall predecease

SAMPLE #1 — Continued

me, then the issue of such deceased child, if any, shall be entitled to the share of their deceased parent, such share to be divided among such issue in equal shares per stirpes. If there are no issue of such deceased child of mine, then the share of such deceased child shall be divided among such of my issue as may be alive at my death in equal shares per stirpes.

V   I HEREBY direct my personal representative that I be buried in a simple manner and that all expenses in connection with my burial be kept to a bare minimum.

VI. I direct that I be buried by the JOHN HIGGINBOTHAM FUNERAL HOME and that all funeral arrangements be made through that funeral home.

VII. I AUTHORIZE AND EMPOWER my personal representative to sell, mortgage and convey all or any part of my real estate or personal estate for cash or for credit or partly for cash and partly for credit at such times, for such amounts and on such terms as my personal representative may deem advisable.

IN WITNESS HEREOF I have to this, my last will and testament, written upon this and the one preceding page of paper, subscribed my name this 15th day of June, 19__.

SIGNED, PUBLISHED, AND DECLARED)
by the said testator, JOHN DAVID)
COOPER, as and for his last will and) _John David Cooper_
testament, in the presence of us, both pre-) JOHN DAVID COOPER
sent at the same time, who, at his request,)
in his presence, and in the presence of)
each other, have subscribed our names as)
witnesses.)

Witness: _Walter Witness_ Witness: _Wanda Witness_
　　　　Walter Witness　　　　　　　　Wanda Witness

Address: 123 View Road　　　　Address: 123 View Road
　　　　Mississauga, Ontario　　　　　Mississauga, Ontario

Occupation: Clerk　　　　Occupation: Mail Carrier

SAMPLE #2
WILL FOR MARRIED PERSON WITH
ADULT CHILDREN ONLY

Sample will for use by a married man or married woman (with children 18 years of age or over) providing for specific bequests. Again, this form is readily adaptable to the married individual with no children or to the unmarried person.

THIS IS THE LAST WILL AND TESTAMENT of me, MARINA ANN SMITH, of the City of Chatham in the County of Kent in the Province of Ontario, Secretary.

I.   I HEREBY REVOKE all wills, codicils, and testamentary dispositions of every nature and kind whatsoever by me heretofore made.

II.   I NOMINATE, CONSTITUTE, AND APPOINT my husband, LAWRENCE JOHN SMITH, to be the sole personal representative of this, my will; provided that should my said husband predecease me, or should he die before the administration of my estate has been completed, or should he be unwilling or unable to act, then I NOMINATE, CONSTITUTE, AND APPOINT my brother, MASSEY GORDON JONES, to be the personal representative of this, my will, in the place and stead of my said husband.

III.   I DIRECT my personal representative to pay my just debts, funeral, and testamentary expenses and all income taxes, estate, inheritance and succession duties, or taxes wheresoever payable.

IV.   I GIVE, DEVISE, AND BEQUEATH all my property of every nature and kind and wheresoever situate, including any property over which I may have a general power of appointment, to my personal representative on the following trusts:

    (a)   I direct my personal representative to pay to my friend, EDWARD ALBERT GREEN, presently residing at 18 Glen Road, Chatham, the sum of TWO HUNDRED AND FIFTY ($250) DOLLARS, for his own use absolutely;

(b) I direct my personal representative to deliver to my daughter, MITZI MAY BROWN, my sterling silver tea service, my wedding ring, and any automobile I may own at the time of my death, for her own use absolutely;

(c) In the event that my said husband, LAWRENCE JOHN SMITH, survives me for a period of thirty days, I direct my personal representative to pay or transfer to him the residue of my estate, for his own use absolutely;

(d) In the event that my said husband shall predecease me or, surviving me, die within a period of thirty days following my decease, I direct my personal representative to divide the residue of my estate equally between my two children, WILLIAM PETER SMITH and MARJORIE JOAN WINTER, for their own use absolutely; provided that should either or both of my said children predecease me, then the issue of any such deceased child, if any, shall be entitled to the share of their deceased parent, such share to be divided among such issue in equal shares per stirpes. If there are no issue of such deceased child of mine, then the share of such deceased child shall be divided among such of my issue as may be alive at my death in equal shares per stirpes.

V.   IF ANY PERSON should become entitled to a share in my estate before attaining the age of eighteen years, the share of such person shall be held and kept invested by my personal representative until he or she attains the age of eighteen years, at which time my personal representative shall pay or transfer to such person the whole of his share together with any income earned thereon, for his or her own use absolutely.

VI. I HEREBY GIVE AND BEQUEATH my eyes to the EYE BANK OF CANADA under the auspices of the CANADIAN NATIONAL INSTITUTE FOR THE BLIND. I hereby confirm the arrangements made by me during my lifetime respecting this bequest of my eyes, and instruct my personal representative to carry out such arrangements.

VII. I AUTHORIZE AND EMPOWER my personal representative to sell, mortgage and convey all or any part of my real estate or personal estate for cash or for credit or partly for cash and partly for credit at such times, for such amounts and on such terms as my personal representative may deem advisable.

IN WITNESS WHEREOF I have to this, my last will and testament, written upon this and the two preceding pages of paper, subscribed my name this 15th day of June, 19__.

SIGNED, PUBLISHED AND DECLARED)
by the said testatrix, MARINA ANN)
SMITH, as and for her last will and testa-) *Marina Ann Smith*
ment, in the presence of us, both present)   MARINA ANN SMITH
at the same time, who, at her request, in)
her presence and in the presence of each)
other, have subscribed our names as wit-)
nesses.)

Witness: *Walter Witness*   Witness: *Wanda Witness*
    Walter Witness   Wanda Witness

Address: 123 View Road   Address: 123 View Road
       Mississauga, Ontario   Mississauga, Ontario
Occupation: Clerk   Occupation: Mail carrier

SAMPLE #3
WILL FOR MARRIED PERSON WITH
INFANT CHILDREN

Sample will for use when children of person making the will are under the age of 18 years. This will incorporates trust provisions for the shares of the infant children.

THIS IS THE LAST WILL AND TESTAMENT of me, GERALD THOMAS PHILLIPS, of the City of Oshawa, in the Regional Municipality of Durham in the Province of Ontario, Peace Officer.

I.   I HEREBY REVOKE all wills, codicils, and testamentary dispositions of every nature and kind whatsoever by me heretofore made.

II.   I NOMINATE, CONSTITUTE, AND APPOINT my brother, RICHARD FRANK PHILLIPS, of 33 Queen Street East, Toronto, to be the sole personal representative and trustee of this, my will; provided that should my said brother predecease me or die before the trusts hereof shall have terminated or should my said brother refuse or be unable to act or continue to act as a personal representative and trustee, then I NOMINATE, CONSTITUTE, AND APPOINT my solicitor, SAMUEL XAVIER SNIDER, to be the personal representative and trustee of this my will in the place and stead of my said brother. I hereinafter refer to my personal representative and trustee, for the time being, as my "trustee."

III.   I GIVE, DEVISE, AND BEQUEATH all my property of every nature and kind and wheresoever situate, including any property over which I may have a general power of appointment, to my trustee upon the following trusts, namely:

(a)   To use his discretion in the realization of my estate, with power to my trustee to sell, call in and convert into money any part of my estate not consisting of money at such time or times, in such manner and upon such terms, and either for cash or credit or for part cash and part credit as my trustee may in his uncontrolled discretion decide upon, or to postpone such conversion of my estate or any part or parts thereof for such length of time as he may think best, and I hereby declare that my trustee may retain any portion of my estate in the form in which it may be at my death (notwithstanding that it may not be in the form of an investment in which trustees are authorized to invest trust funds, and whether or not there is a liability attached to any such portion of my estate) for such length of time as my trustee may in his absolute discretion deem advisable, and my trustee shall not be held responsible for any loss that may happen to my estate by reason of his so doing;

(b) To pay my just debts, funeral, and testamentary expenses and all income taxes, estate, inheritance and succession duties, or taxes whether imposed by or pursuant to the law of this or any other jurisdiction whatsoever that may be payable in connection with any property passing (or deemed so to pass by any governing law) on my death or in connection with any gift or benefit given or conferred by me either during my lifetime or by survivorship or by this my will or any codicil thereto and whether such duties or taxes be payable in respect of estates or interests which fall into possession at my death or at any subsequent time; and I hereby authorize my trustee to commute or prepay any such taxes or duties.

(c) To pay to my sister, JOANNE MARIE PHILLIPS, presently residing in Fort Lauderdale, Florida, the sum of TWENTY THOUSAND ($20 000) DOLLARS, for her own use absolutely;

(d) To pay to the YONGE STREET MISSION, Toronto, the sum of ONE THOUSAND ($1 000) DOLLARS, to be used for its general purposes. I declare that the receipt of the person purporting to be the treasurer or charged with the duties normally performed by a treasurer shall be sufficient discharge to my trustee, and I declare that my trustee shall have no obligation to see to the uses to which such sum is put;

(e) To pay or transfer the residue of my estate to my wife, MARILYN LEE PHILLIPS, if she survives me for a period of thirty days, for her own use absolutely;

(f) In the event that my wife shall predecease me, or surviving me shall die within a period of thirty days following my decease, then on the death of the survivor of me and my wife, to divide the residue of my estate into as many equal shares as there shall be children of mine alive at the death of the survivor of me and my wife, and I will and declare that if any child of mine shall then be dead but shall have left issue him or her surviving and then alive, such deceased child of mine shall be considered as alive for the purpose of such division.

My trustee shall set aside one of such equal shares for each child of mine who shall be living at the death of the survivor of me and my wife and shall keep such share invested and apply so much of the net income therefrom and so much of the capital thereof as my trustee shall in his uncontrolled discretion consider advisable from time to time for the benefit of such child until he or she attains the age of eighteen years when such share or the amount thereof remaining shall be paid or transferred to him or her absolutely. If such child should die before becoming entitled to receive the whole of his or her share in my estate, such share or the amount thereof remaining shall be held by my trustee in trust for the issue of such child who survive him or her in equal shares per stirpes. If such child should leave no issue him or her surviving, such share or the amount thereof remaining shall be held by my trustee in trust for my issue alive at the death of such child in equal shares per stirpes.

My trustee shall set aside one of such equal shares for the issue of each child of mine who shall have predeceased the survivor of me and my wife leaving issue alive at the death of the survivor of me and my wife and shall divide such share among the issue of such deceased child then alive in equal shares per stirpes.

SAMPLE #3 — Continued

IV. NOTWITHSTANDING anything herein contained, if any person should become entitled to any share in my estate before attaining the age of eighteen, the share of such person shall be held and kept invested by my trustee and so much of the net income therefrom and so much of the capital thereof as my trustee in his uncontrolled discretion considers necessary or advisable shall be used for the benefit of such person until he or she attains the age of eighteen.

V. I AUTHORIZE my trustee to make any payments for any person under the age of majority to a parent or guardian of such person whose receipt shall be a sufficient discharge to my trustee, and my trustee shall not be obligated to see to the application thereof.

VI. TO FACILITATE THE ADMINISTRATION of my estate by my trustee, I declare that, in addition to the powers herein before vested in him by this will, and in addition to all powers conferred upon trustees by law or by the Trustee Act, my trustee when making investments for my estate shall not be limited to investments authorized by law for trustees, but may make any investments which in his absolute discretion he considers advisable and in the best interests of my estate, and my trustee shall not be held responsible for any loss that may happen to my estate by reason of his so doing.

VII. ANY REFERENCE in this my will or any codicil hereto to a person in terms of a relationship to another person determined by blood or marriage shall not include a person born outside of marriage or a person who comes within the description traced through another person who was born outside of marriage, provided that any person who has been legally adopted shall be regarded as having been born in lawful wedlock to his or her adopting parent.

VIII. ANY benefit, whether as to income or capital or both, or income from capital to which any person shall become entitled in accordance with the provisions of this my will or any codicil thereto, shall not fall into any community of property which may exist between any such person and his or her spouse and shall not form part of his or her net family property for any purpose or purposes of the *Family Law Act, 1986,* in the province of Ontario and any amendments thereto or any successor legislation thereto, but shall only be paid

SAMPLE #3 — Continued

by my trustee to such person on the condition that the same shall remain the separate property of such person, free from the control of his or her spouse. The separate receipt of such person shall be a discharge to my trustee in respect of any such payment.

IX.   IN THE EVENT that my wife predeceases me and any child of mine is under the age of 18 years, at the time of my death, I nominate, constitute, and appoint my sister, VALERIE PHILLIPS, to have custody of such child and be the guardian of such child's property during his or her minority.

IN TESTIMONY WHEREOF I have to this, my last will and testament, written upon this and the four preceding pages of paper, subscribed my name this 16th day of June, 19__.

SIGNED, PUBLISHED, AND DECLARED   )
by the said testator, GERALD THOMAS   )
PHILLIPS, as and for his last will and   )
testament, in the presence of us, both pre-)   *G. Thomas Phillips*
sent at the same time, who at his, GER-   )   G. THOMAS PHILLIPS
ALD THOMAS PHILLIPS, request, in his   )
presence and in the presence of each   )
other, have subscribed our names as wit-)
nesses.   )

Witness: *Walter Witness*   Witness: *Wanda Witness*
             Walter Witness   Wanda Witness

Address: 123 View Road   Address: 123 View Road
            Mississauga, Ontario   Mississauga, Ontario
Occupation: Clerk   Occupation: Mail carrier

SAMPLE #4
A CODICIL

THIS IS THE FIRST CODICIL to the last will of me, MARY DOE, of the City of Toronto in the Municipality of Metropolitan Toronto in the Province of Ontario, which said last will bears the date of the 13th day of May, 1984.

I.   I HEREBY REVOKE Clause III(b) of my said last will and testament.

II. I HEREBY REVOKE Clause III(f) of my said last will and testament and substitute therefore the following provision:

"(f) I direct my trustee to deliver to my aunt, QUEENIE DOE, my sterling silver goblet."

III. IN ALL OTHER RESPECTS I confirm my said will.

IN WITNESS WHEREOF I have to this first codicil to my last will, written upon this one page of paper, subscribed my name this 23rd day of June, 19__.

SIGNED, PUBLISHED, AND DE-)
CLARED by the said testatrix, MARY)
DOE, as and for a codicil to her last will,) *Mary Doe*
in the presence of us, both present at the) ─────────────
same time, who at her request, in her)   MARY DOE
presence and in the presence of each)
other, have hereunto subscribed our)
names as witnesses.)

Witness: *Walter Witness*   Witness: *Wanda Witness*
Walter Witness   Wanda Witness
Address: 123 View Road   Address: 123 View Road
         Mississauga, Ontario   Mississauga, Ontario
Occupation: Clerk   Occupation: Mail carrier

3

PROBATE

This chapter deals with the steps to be taken on death, i.e., the steps involved in the administration of an estate. This does not necessarily mean that after reading the book, you will be qualified to administer an estate without legal counsel. Rather, it is hoped that you will develop an understanding of the basic procedures involved and whether legal counsel is needed. In small, uncomplicated estates, you may be able to complete properly the various returns and applications required when an individual dies. However, you should first consult *Probate Guide for Ontario,* another book in the Self-Counsel Series, for a more detailed examination of how to administer an estate.

In this chapter you will find samples of the forms generally filed by the personal representative following the death of the testator in a hypothetical case. This book cannot and does not attempt to deal with every possible problem that may arise in a particular estate situation.

a. WHAT IS PROBATE?

Before entering a lengthy discussion of the duties of a personal representative in the administration of an estate, it is necessary to define some terms.

Probate is the procedure by which the will of the deceased person is approved by the court as a valid and last will of the deceased. It also confirms the appointment of the person named in the will as personal representative. The procedure is not required to validate the will or to effect the appointment of the executor. It merely confirms the validity and appointment.

The Application for Certificate of Appointment of Estate Trustee With a Will is made to the Ontario Court (General Division) of the county or region in which the deceased lived at the time of death. If the deceased did not reside in Ontario at the time of death, application can be made to the court of any county or region in which assets of the deceased were situated at the time of death. The application is made by the personal representative named in the will or by a lawyer retained by the personal representative. The application does not involve a personal appearance in court, but various documents are submitted to the court along with the original signed copy of the last will of the deceased. The samples in this chapter illustrate the various documents which would be filed by the personal representative in our hypothetical estate. Forms for this purpose may be obtained from all legal stationers or from Self-Counsel Press.

1. Application for Certificate of Appointment of Estate Trustee With a Will

This form (see Sample #5) is the official application submitted to the court outlining information about the deceased, including his or her place of residence, marital status, and date of death. This form must be signed by the estate trustee.

The upper portion provides details of the deceased, the lower portion provides details of the value of the estate, and the second page gives details of the applicant or applicants (those named in the will as personal representative(s)). The second page of the form is actually an affidavit to be sworn under oath by the applicant.

2. Notice of the Application for a Certificate of Appointment and Affidavit of Service of Notice

It is necessary to send each person who is entitled to a share of the estate a Notice of An Application for a Certificate of

Appointment (see Sample #6), together with a copy of the will. In order to satisfy the court that you have complied with this requirement, you must complete an Affidavit of Service of Notice (see Sample #7). The affidavit is completed by inserting the name of the applicant who served the notice. It is then signed in the presence of a notary or commissioner for taking oaths and filed in court with the other documents that accompany your application.

3. Certificate of Appointment of Estate Trustee With a Will

This is the document which grants probate of the will to the executor named in it. It is prepared by the applicant and submitted to the court to be signed and sealed by the Registrar (see Sample #8).

4. Affidavit of Execution of Will or Codicil

This is an affidavit made by one of the witnesses to a will or codicil (in the case of a will that is not a holograph will) confirming under oath that the person making the affidavit was present, with the other witness, when the will or codicil was signed. Only one of the two witnesses need sign such an affidavit. (See Sample #9.)

If neither of the witnesses is living or if neither can be found, the propriety of the signing of the will can be established in other ways. An affidavit would have to be filed with the court to establish that both witnesses are dead or cannot be found. Then, a further affidavit (somewhat similar to that filed in connection with a holograph will) must be made by someone familiar with the deceased's handwriting. This affidavit establishes that the signature on the will is that of the testator.

Sample #10 shows the Affidavit Attesting to the Handwriting and Signature of a Holograph Will or Codicil. Again, the form is very simple and should be sworn by someone very familiar with the deceased's handwriting.

SAMPLE #5
APPLICATION FOR CERTIFICATE OF
APPOINTMENT OF ESTATE TRUSTEE WITH A WILL

Ontario Court (General Division)
at

**APPLICATION FOR CERTIFICATE OF
APPOINTMENT OF ESTATE TRUSTEE
WITH A WILL (INDIVIDUAL APPLICANT)**
Form 74.4 under the Rules (Page 1 of 2)

This application is filed by *(insert name and address)*

MARY MATILDA SMITH, 42 ROSE AVENUE, TORONTO

DETAILS ABOUT THE DECEASED PERSON

Name *(insert surname and forename(s), and, if applicable, any other name by which the deceased person was known)*

SMITH, JOHN ADAMS

Address of fixed place of abode *(street or postal address) (city or town)*	*(county, district, regional or metropolitan municipality)*
42 ROSE AVENUE, TORONTO	MUNICIPALITY OF METROPOLITAN TORONTO

If the deceased person had no fixed place of abode in Ontario, did he or she have property in Ontario? ☐ No ☐ Yes	Last occupation of deceased person
	TRUCK DRIVER

Place of death *(city or town; county, district, regional or metropolitan municipality)*	**Date of death** *(day, month, year)*	**Date of last will** *(marked as Exhibit "A") (day, month, year)*
TORONTO, MUNICIPALITY OF METROPOLITAN TORONTO	13 APRIL 199–	13 APRIL, 1980

Was the deceased person 18 years of age or older at the date of the will (or 21 years of age or older if the will is dated earlier than September 1, 1971)? ☐ No ☒ Yes
If not, explain why certificate is being sought. Give details in an attached schedule.

Date of codicil *(marked as Exhibit "B") (day, month, year)*	**Date of codicil** *(marked as Exhibit "C") (day, month, year)*
NONE	NONE

Date of codicil *(marked as Exhibit "D") (day, month, year)*	**Date of codicil** *(marked as Exhibit "E") (day, month, year)*
NONE	NONE
	(additional codicils may be described in an attached schedule and marked as exhibits)

Marital status	Did the deceased person marry after the date of the will? ☒ No ☐ Yes
☐ Unmarried ☐ Widowed	If yes, explain why certificate is being sought.
☒ Married ☐ Divorced	Give details in an attached schedule.

Was a marriage of the deceased person terminated by a judgment absolute of divorce, or declared a nullity, after the date of the will? ☒ No ☐ Yes If yes, give details in an attached schedule.	Is any person who signed the will or a codicil as witness or for the testator, or the spouse of such a person, a beneficiary under the will? ☒ No ☐ Yes If yes, give details in an attached schedule.

VALUE OF ASSETS OF ESTATE

Do not include in the total amount: insurance payable to a named beneficiary or assigned for value, property held jointly and passing by survivorship, or real estate outside Ontario.

Personal property	Real estate, net of encumbrances	Total
$ 58,796.80	$ nil	$58,796.80

Is there any person entitled to an interest in the estate who is not an applicant?
☐ No ☒ Yes

If a person named in the will as estate trustee is not an applicant, explain.

If a person not named in the will or a codicil as estate trustee is an applicant, explain why that person is entitled to apply.

SAMPLE #5 — Continued

APPLICATION FOR CERTIFICATE OF APPOINTMENT
OF ESTATE TRUSTEE WITH A WILL (INDIVIDUAL APPLICANT)
Form 74.4 under the Rules (Page 2 of 2)

AFFIDAVIT(S) OF APPLICANT(S)
(Attach a separate sheet for additional affidavits, if necessary.)

I, an applicant named in this application, make oath and say/affirm:

1. I am 18 years of age or older.

2. The exhibit(s) referred to in this application are the last will and each codicil (where applicable) of the deceased person and I do not know of any later will or codicil.

3. I will faithfully administer the deceased person's property according to law and render a complete and true account of my administration when lawfully required.

4. If I am not named as estate trustee in the will or codicil, consents of persons who together have a majority interest in the value of the assets of the estate at the date of death are attached.

5. The information contained in this application and in any attached schedules is true, to the best of my knowledge and belief.

Name *(surname and forename(s))*	**Occupation**
SMITH MARY MATILDA	WAITRESS

Address *(street or postal address)*	*(city or town)*	*(province)*	*(postal code)*
42 ROSE AVENUE,	TORONTO	ONTARIO	M9A 2C6

Sworn/Affirmed before me at the City
of   Toronto
in the   Municipality
of   Metropolitan Toronto
this   day of   March   , 199–

A Commissioner for Taking Affidavits *(or as may be)*	Signature of applicant MARY MATILDA SMITH

Name *(surname and forename(s))*	**Occupation**

Address *(street or postal address)*	*(city or town)*	*(province)*	*(postal code)*

Sworn/Affirmed before me at the
of
in the
of
this   day of   , 19

A Commissioner for Taking Affidavits *(or as may be)*	Signature of applicant

Name *(surname and forename(s))*	**Occupation**

Address *(street or postal address)*	*(city or town)*	*(province)*	*(postal code)*

Sworn/Affirmed before me at the
of
in the
of
this   day of   , 19

A Commissioner for Taking Affidavits *(or as may be)*	Signature of applicant

SAMPLE #6
NOTICE OF AN APPLICATION FOR A CERTIFICATE OF APPOINTMENT OF ESTATE TRUSTEE WITH A WILL*

ONTARIO COURT (GENERAL DIVISION)

NOTICE OF AN APPLICATION FOR A CERTIFICATE OF APPOINTMENT OF ESTATE TRUSTEE WITH A WILL

(insert name) **IN THE ESTATE OF** JOHN ADAMS SMITH , **deceased.**

(insert date) **1.** The deceased died on APRIL 13, 199–

2. Attached to this notice are:

(A) If the notice is sent to or in respect of a person entitled only to a specified item of property or stated amount of money, an extract of the part or parts of the will or codicil relating to the gift, or a copy of the will (and codicil(s), if any).

(B) If the notice is sent to or in respect of any other beneficiary, a copy of the will (and codicil(s), if any).

(C) If the notice is sent to the Children's Lawyer or the Public Guardian and Trustee, a copy of the will (and codicil(s), if any) and a statement of the estimated value of the interest of the person represented.

3. The applicant named in this notice is applying for a certificate of appointment of estate trustee with a will.

APPLICANT

NAME	ADDRESS
MARY MATILDA SMITH	42 ROSE AVENUE TORONTO, ONTARIO

4. The following charities are entitled to share in the distribution of the estate:

Name	Address
NONE	

* A copy of the above notice must be sent to each person who is entitled to a share of the estate along with a copy of the will.

53

SAMPLE #6 — Continued

5. The following persons who are less than 18 years of age are entitled to share in the distribution of the estate:

Name	Date of birth *(Day, Month, Year)*	Name and address of parent or guardian
	N/A	

6. The following persons who are mentally incapable within the meaning of section 6 of the *Substitute Decisions Act, 1992* in respect of an issue in the proceeding, and who have guardians or attorneys acting under powers of attorney with authority to act in the proceeding, are entitled to share in the distribution of the estate:

Name and address of person	Name and address of guardian or attorney* *Specify whether guardian or attorney.*
	NONE

7. The following persons who are mentally incapable within the meaning of section 6 of the *Substitute Decisions Act, 1992* in respect of an issue in the proceeding, and who do not have guardians or attorneys acting under powers of attorney with authority to act in the proceeding, are entitled to share in the distribution of the estate:

Name and address of person

NONE

SAMPLE #6 — Continued

(Delete if inapplicable.)

8. Unborn or unascertained persons may be entitled to share in the distribution of the estate.

9. All other persons entitled to share in the distribution of the estate are as follows:

Name	Address
MARY MATILDA SMITH	42 ROSE AVENUE TORONTO, ONTARIO
EDWARD SMITH	42 FIRST STREET TORONTO, ONTARIO

10. This notice is being sent, by regular lettermail, to all adult persons and charities named in this notice (except to an applicant who is entitled to share in the distribution of the estate), to the Public Guardian and Trustee if paragraph 4 or 7 applies, to a parent or guardian of the minor and to the Children's Lawyer if paragraph 5 applies, to the guardian or attorney if paragraph 6 applies, and to the Children's Lawyer if paragraph 8 applies.

DATE MARCH 18, 199-

SAMPLE #7
AFFIDAVIT OF SERVICE OF NOTICE

AFFIDAVIT OF SERVICE OF NOTICE (WITH A WILL)
(Form 74.6 under the Rules)
Amended OCTOBER 1996

ONTARIO COURT (GENERAL DIVISION)

(insert name) **IN THE ESTATE OF**   JOHN ADAMS SMITH   , deceased.

AFFIDAVIT OF SERVICE OF NOTICE

(insert name)   **I,**   MARY MATILDA SMITH

(insert city or town and county or district, metropolitan or regional municipality of residence)   **of**   THE CITY OF TORONTO, IN THE MUNICIPALITY OF METROPOLITAN TORONTO

make oath and say/affirm:

1.   I am an applicant for a certificate of appointment of estate trustee with a will in the estate.

2.   I have sent or caused to be sent a notice in Form 74.7, a copy of which is marked as Exhibit "A" to this affidavit, to all adult persons and charities named in the notice (except to an applicant who is entitled to share in the distribution of the estate), to the Public Guardian and Trustee if paragraph 4 or 7 of the notice applies, to a parent or guardian of the minor and to the Children's Lawyer if paragraph 5 applies, to the guardian or attorney if paragraph 6 applies, and to the Children's Lawyer if paragraph 8 applies, all by regular lettermail sent to the person's last known address.

3.   I attached or caused to be attached to each notice the following:
   (A) In the case of a notice sent to or in respect of a person entitled only to a specified item of property or stated amount of money, an extract of the part or parts of the will or codicil relating to the gift, or a copy of the will (and codicil(s), if any).
   (B) In the case of a notice sent to or in respect of any other beneficiary, a copy of the will (and codicil(s) if any).
   (C) In the case of a notice sent to the Children's Lawyer or the Public Guardian and Trustee, a copy of the will (and codicil(s), if any) and a statement of the estimated value of the interest of the person respresented.

4.   To the best of my knowledge and belief, the persons named in the notice are all the persons who are entitled to share in the distribution of the estate.

SWORN/AFFIRMED BEFORE me at the City
of   Toronto
in the Municipality
of   Metropolitan Toronto
this   23rd day of   February   , 199–

                                                   MARY MATILDA SMITH

_____
A Commissioner for Taking Affidavits
(or as may be)

SAMPLE #8
CERTIFICATE OF APPOINTMENT OF ESTATE TRUSTEE WITH A WILL

CERTIFICATE OF APPOINTMENT OF
ESTATE TRUSTEE WITH A WILL
(Form 74.13 under the Rules)

Court file no.

ONTARIO COURT
(GENERAL DIVISION)

IN THE ESTATE OF   JOHN ADAMS SMITH   , deceased,

late of THE CITY OF TORONTO, MUNICIPALITY OF METROPOLITAN TORONTO

occupation   TRUCK DRIVER

who died on   APRIL 13TH, 199-

CERTIFICATE OF APPOINTMENT
OF ESTATE TRUSTEE WITH A WILL

Applicant	Address	Occupation
MARY MATILDA SMITH	42 ROSE AVENUE CITY OF TORONTO MUNICIPALITY OF METROPOLITAN TORONTO	WAITRESS

This CERTIFICATE OF APPOINTMENT OF ESTATE TRUSTEE WITH A WILL is hereby issued under the seal of the court to the applicant named above. A copy of the deceased's last will (and codicil(s), if any) is attached.

DATE   199-

JB Registrar
Registrar

Address of court office

361 UNIVERSITY AVENUE,
TORONTO, ONTARIO

SAMPLE #9
AFFIDAVIT OF EXECUTION OF WILL OR CODICIL

AFFIDAVIT OF EXECUTION OF WILL OR CODICIL
(Form 74 8 under the Rules)

ONTARIO COURT (GENERAL DIVISION)

In the matter of the execution of a will or codicil of   JOHN ADAMS SMITH
(insert name)

AFFIDAVIT

I,   JAMES GORDON PETERS,
(insert name)

Toronto,
of 1444 Logan Street, City of Toronto, Municipality of Metropolitan/
(insert city or town and county or district, metropolitan or regional municipality of residence)

make oath and say/affirm:

1. On   April 13th, 1980,   , I was present and saw the document marked as
(date)
Exhibit "A" to this affidavit executed by   JOHN ADAMS SMITH
(insert name)

2. JOHN ADAMS SMITH   executed the document in the presence of
(insert name)
Metropolitan Toronto,
myself and MARY A. McGRATH, of the City of Toronto, Municipality of / .
(insert name of other witness and city or town, county or district, metropolitan or regional municipality of residence)

We were both present at the same time, and signed the document in the testator's presence as attesting witnesses.

SWORN/AFFIRMED BEFORE me at the   City
of   Toronto
in the   Municipality
of   Metropolitan Toronto   *James Gordon Peters*
this 18th day of   March   ,199   JAMES GORDON PETERS

88 Commissioner
A Commissioner for Taking Affidavits
(or as may be)

NOTE: If the testator was blind or signed by making his or her mark, add the following paragraph:
3.   Before its execution, the document was read over to the testator, who (was blind) (signed by making his or her mark). The testator appeared to understand the contents.

WARNING: A beneficiary or the spouse of a beneficiary should not be a witness.

58

SAMPLE #10
AFFIDAVIT ATTESTING TO THE HANDWRITING AND SIGNATURE OF A HOLOGRAPH WILL OR CODICIL

AFFIDAVIT ATTESTING TO THE HANDWRITING
AND SIGNATURE OF A HOLOGRAPH WILL OR CODICIL
(Form 74.9 under the Rules)

ONTARIO COURT (GENERAL DIVISION)

IN THE ESTATE OF   JOSEPH PETERSON   , deceased.
(insert name)

AFFIDAVIT ATTESTING TO THE HANDWRITING AND SIGNATURE OF A HOLOGRAPH WILL OR CODICIL

I,   MARIA V.F. SERPA
(insert name)

of the City of Toronto, in the Municipality of Metropolitan Toronto
(insert city or town and county or district, metropolitan or regional municipality of residence)

make oath and say / affirm:

1. I was well acquainted with the deceased and have frequently seen the deceased's signature and handwriting.

2. I believe the whole of the document dated   January 1st, 1987   , now
(insert date)

shown to me and marked as Exhibit "A" to this affidavit, including the signature, is in the handwriting of the deceased.

SWORN / AFFIRMED BEFORE me at the City

of   Toronto

in the   Municipality

of Metropolitan Toronto

this 10th day of   June   , 19 9

Maria VF Serpa
MARIA V.F. SERPA

J.B. Commissioner
A Commissioner for Taking Affidavits
(or as may be)

59

In addition to the forms outlined above, the original and one photocopy of the will (and codicil, if any) must also be submitted to the court. The last page of the will, the page upon which the signatures appear, is turned over and on the back, reference is made to the fact that the will is an exhibit to each form. This is also where it will be marked for identification and signed by the personal representative. See Sample #11 for the wording used to accomplish this.

After the documents are properly signed and sworn, one copy of each, along with the will, is delivered to the office of the court for the particular county or region. The fee is $5 for every $1 000 of estate assets up to $50 000, and $15 for every $1 000 of estate assets over $50 000.

The amount of probate fees being charged by the Ontario government has been called into question. In October 1998, the Supreme Court of Canada ruled that the probate fees violate the constitution of Canada because they do not reflect the costs of operating the probate court and are actually a form of indirect taxation. The Supreme Court has allowed the government a period of six months to bring its probate fees in line with the constitution. It remains to be seen whether this will result in a reduction in probate fees, or whether new legislation will be passed to validate the existing fee structure.

Any property (whether real estate, furniture, stocks and bonds, or a bank account) held in the joint names of two individuals does not form a part of the estate of a joint owner who dies. The law provides that any such property held in joint names passes automatically to the surviving joint owner and does not form part of the estate of the deceased and is, therefore, not affected by the will if one is left or by the intestacy provisions of the Succession Law Reform Act if a joint owner dies without a will. Thus, the value of any joint property is excluded from the totals when declaring the value of the estate.

Life insurance which is payable directly to a named beneficiary is paid directly to the named individual and is not considered an asset of the deceased's estate for probate purposes. Again, the proceeds of any such policies are ignored in the Application for Certificate of Estate Trustee.

Finally, any real estate owned by the deceased and situated outside of Ontario is not included in the value of the estate. For real estate situated within Ontario, only the net value of the real estate (after deducting the amount of any mortgages outstanding) is included in the value of the estate. Other debts of the deceased or the estate are not, however, deducted when calculating the value of the estate.

Once the court fees have been paid and the documents checked, the Certificate of Appointment of Estate Trustee is issued by the court. This is the name given to the court document which confirms the validity of the will and the appointment of the personal representative.

It should be observed that it is not always necessary to probate the will of a deceased person. If the estate is small or the assets are of such a nature that probate is not required, the named personal representative may be able to administer the estate by simply providing copies of the will to those with whom he or she must deal, rather than furnishing copies of the Certificate of Appointment of Estate Trustee.

b. HOW TO TRANSFER THE DECEASED'S PROPERTY

Notarized copies of the Certificate of Appointment of Estate Trustee will be required by the personal representative to transfer property registered in the name of the deceased.

If bonds or stocks form part of the estate, the transfer agent will demand from the personal representative a notarized copy of the Certificate before transferring bonds or stocks from the name of the deceased. The transfer agent will often demand to examine the original Certificate as well.

SAMPLE #11
WILL WITH PERSONAL REPRESENTATIVE'S NOTATIONS ON BACK

THIS IS THE LAST WILL AND TESTAMENT of me, JOHN ADAMS SMITH, of the City of Toronto, in the Municipality of Metropolitan Toronto, and Province of Ontario, Truck Driver.

1.   I HEREBY REVOKE all wills, codicils, and testamentary dispositions of every nature and kind whatsoever by me heretofore made.

2.   I NOMINATE, CONSTITUTE, AND APPOINT my wife, MARY MATILDA SMITH, to be the personal representative and trustee of this, my will.

3.   I GIVE, DEVISE, AND BEQUEATH all my property of every nature and kind and wheresoever situate, including any property over which I may have a general power of appointment, to my said wife, MARY MATILDA SMITH, for her own use absolutely.

IN TESTIMONY WHEREOF I have to this my last will and testament written upon this single page of paper subscribed my name this 13th day of April, 19__.

SIGNED, PUBLISHED, AND DECLARED)
by the said testator, JOHN ADAMS)
SMITH, as and for his last will and testa-)
ment, in the presence of us, both present) *John Adams Smith*
at the same time, who, at his JOHN) JOHN ADAMS SMITH
ADAMS SMITH request, in his presence)
and in the presence of each other, have)
hereunto subscribed our names as wit-)
nesses.)

Witness: *James G. Peters* Witness: *Mary A. McGrath*
James G. Peters   Mary A. McGrath
Address: 456 Main Avenue   Address: 23 Central Lane
         Mississauga, Ontario   Mississauga, Ontario
Occupation: Clerk   Occupation: Mail carrier

REVERSE SIDE OF SIGNING PAGE OF WILL

This is the last will and testament of JOHN ADAMS SMITH, marked by me for identification.

Mary Matilda Smith
Personal representative

This is Exhibit "A" to the affidavit of James G. Peters sworn before me this 18th day of June, 19__.

J.M. Commissioner
A Commissioner for taking oaths in and for the province of Ontario.

This is Exhibit "A" to the affidavit of Mary A. McGrath sworn before me this 18th day of June, 19__.

J.M. Commissioner
A Commissioner for taking oaths in and for the province of Ontario.

If real estate or mortgages are included among the assets of the estate, a notarized copy of the Certificate of Appointment of Estate Trustee must be registered in the Land Registry Office for the county or region in which the property the deceased owned or held a mortgage is located. For more information see *Probate Guide for Ontario,* another book in the Self-Counsel Series, where details of how to transfer estate assets are set forth.

c. POWERS AND DUTIES OF THE PERSONAL REPRESENTATIVE

A personal representative has many duties and obligations towards the estate. He or she must prepare an inventory of all the assets of the estate (see Sample #12) and a list of all the debts; protect the assets of the estate until able to transfer them to the beneficiaries; file the deceased's income tax return for the year of death and any other tax returns not previously filed by the deceased; pay all debts of the deceased and creditors of the estate; distribute the estate to the beneficiaries entitled; and account to the beneficiaries for his or her handling of the estate. The checklist contained later in this chapter gives a more detailed list of items for which the personal representative is responsible.

A personal representative has the duty to arrange for the burial of the deceased and, accordingly, has the power to incur reasonable funeral expenses. If the funeral expenses are excessive, the personal representative may be obliged to pay personally for the excess. Reasonable funeral expenses can be paid out of the estate's assets. What is "reasonable" varies from estate to estate, but it depends for a large part on the deceased's station in life.

The personal representative has the power and duty to examine all the personal papers of the deceased. This may be necessary in order to track down all the assets and debts of the deceased.

SAMPLE #12
A LIST OF ASSETS

John Adams Smith died on June 1, 19___ in an automobile accident. John was employed as a truck driver for Gordon Green Transport Ltd. John was 30. He is survived by his wife, Mary, and three small children, Joanne, Peter, and Gloria. John had a simple will prepared in April of 1979 naming Mary as executrix and leaving everything to her. Following is a list of assets which belonged to John at the time of death, including insurance policies payable on account of his death:

(1) House located at 42 Rose Avenue, Toronto, owned jointly with wife, Mary

(2) A mortgage on 99 Michigan Row, in the township of Raleigh

(3) A $20 000 life insurance policy on John with Everyman's Insurance Society of Windsor, payable to John's estate

(4) A $10 000 life insurance policy on John with Canadian Life and Indemnity Corporation, payable to Mary Smith

(5) Bank account with United Bank of Canada

(6) Account with Independent Credit Union

(7) Cash in wallet of $77.24

(8) Canada Savings Bonds of $6 000

(9) Intercolonial Pipe Lines debentures of $10 000

(10) 12 shares of Rainbow Gold Mines Ltd.

(11) 100 shares of Gordon Lumber Inc.

(12) 3 shares of Bell Communications of New Brunswick Limited

(13) 1984 Chevrolet automobile

(14) Household goods and furniture

(15) Miscellaneous jewellery

The personal representative has the power to take possession of all the assets and possessions of the deceased person. Whether or not he or she has the power to sell or otherwise dispose of the assets of the estate depends in part upon whether or not this power is given in the will. To the extent that the assets must be sold to pay debts of the deceased or to pay expenses of the administration of the estate, the personal representative has the power to sell automatically.

A personal representative is well advised to publish in a local newspaper a notice to creditors and others who have a claim against the estate. The practice has developed of having the notice inserted on three separate occasions, the insertions being one week apart. The notice should be placed in a newspaper published in the region where the deceased lived prior to death. The notice that would be inserted by the personal representative of our hypothetical estate is shown in Sample #13.

The notice should allow from two to four weeks from the date of the final insertion as the time limit within which claims against the estate must be filed.

SAMPLE #13
NOTICE TO CREDITORS AND OTHERS

IN THE ESTATE OF JOHN ADAMS SMITH, late of 42 Rose Avenue in the City of Toronto.

All persons having claims against the estate of JOHN ADAMS SMITH, late of 42 Rose Avenue in the city of Toronto who died on or about the 1st day of June, 19__ are hereby required to send full particulars of such claims to the undersigned personal representative on or before the 28th day of July, 19__, after which date the estate's assets will be distributed having regard only to claims that have then been received and the undersigned will not be liable to any person of whose claim she shall not then have notice.

MARY MATILDA SMITH

---

d. FEES OF PERSONAL REPRESENTATIVES AND LAWYERS

Both the personal representative and any lawyer retained to act for him or her in handling the estate are entitled to a fee from the assets of the estate. Each is entitled to be reimbursed for any money spent in performing his or her duties, as well.

A personal representative is generally entitled to a fee of 5% of the value of the estate. If the administration of the estate involves holding and investing the assets over a period of years, he or she is also entitled to 5% of the income earned by investment of estate assets. On occasion a further two-fifths percent of the value of that portion of the estate being held and invested is also allowed as additional compensation by way of a management fee.

These fees are allowed to the personal representatives as a group if there is more than one. It is up to the group to decide how the compensation should be split between them. The court will assist them if a dispute arises.

The fees for the normal legal services rendered by a lawyer in the administration of an estate will depend in part on the aggregate value of the estate. Traditionally, the scale recommended by the County of York Law Association (which includes all of Metropolitan Toronto) has been as follows:

(a) On the first $10 000 or a portion thereof, 3% of the value of the estate (minimum $500)

(b) On the next $90 000 or a portion thereof, 2%

(c) On the next $200 000 or a portion thereof, 1¼%

(d) On the next $400 000 or portion thereof, ½% of the amount

(e) On the excess over $700 000, additional fees may be charged on the basis of the time involved, the results achieved, and the value of the estate.

These are the recommended amounts for estates of average complexity. If extraordinary problems are encountered, the fee may be higher. If you feel that a lawyer is overcharging, it is always possible to have the account "assessed." This is a legal proceeding whereby a court official confirms the fairness of the account or reduces it to an amount he or she feels is reasonable. Legal fees may also be reviewed by the court at the time the personal representative puts the accounts before the judge for approval.

e. PERSONAL REPRESENTATIVE'S CHECKLIST

The following is a checklist which may be of value in administering an estate. Some of the items have already been discussed, and the rest will be dealt with later in the book. This list is by no means comprehensive. It should merely serve as a guideline to anyone involved in the task of administering an estate. Each particular estate situation will vary and new considerations will enter the picture. The number of items in this list and the complexity of many of these items will illustrate the value of legal assistance in the administration of an estate.

(a) Make all funeral arrangements and attend to burial of deceased.

(b) Locate all bank accounts of deceased. Obtain information about the balance on deposit and notify bank of the death.

(c) Locate all insurance policies and obtain information about the amount payable on each. Notify the insurer of the death.

(d) List the contents of deceased's safety deposit box.

(e) Completely review all personal papers of the deceased in order to locate all assets and debts.

(f) Prepare a detailed inventory of deceased's assets and debts.

(g) Arrange for storage of any assets requiring it. Advise insurers of any physical assets of the deceased. Arrange any insurance coverage required.

(h) Notify the beneficiaries of the death, and send them a Notice of an Application for Certificate of Appointment of Estate Trustee.

(i) Arrange with post office for mail to be re-addressed, if necessary.

(j) Cancel any subscriptions or charge accounts. Return or destroy charge cards.

(k) Obtain all unpaid wages and other benefits from former employer. See all service or veterans' clubs for death benefits that may be payable to estate.

(l) Apply to Ontario Court (General Division) for Certificate of Appointment of Estate Trustee.

(m) Advertise for creditors, if necessary.

(n) File income tax return for year of death and any former years not yet filed by deceased.

(o) Make all reasonable enquiries for persons who may be entitled to a share of the estate by reason of an illegitimate relationship.

(p) Apply for Canada Pension Plan benefits, if any.

(q) Apply for any amounts payable to the estate under insurance policies.

(r) Pay funeral expenses, income taxes payable, and all debts of deceased.

(s) Obtain income tax refund, if any.

(t) Sell any estate assets which must be sold or those which the personal representative chooses to sell if he or she has the power.

(u) Pay money bequests and distribute other property in accordance with instructions in the will (being sure to retain sufficient cash to carry out the final steps).

(v) File the estate's income tax return and pay any tax owing (i.e., if the estate earned any income following the death of the deceased).

(w) Pay legal fees and any outstanding fees relating to the administration of the estate, including compensation for the personal representative.

(x) Obtain releases from all beneficiaries or pass estate accounts before a judge of the court.

(y) Distribute the balance of the estate assets to the rightful beneficiaries.

4

ADMINISTRATION

a. WHAT IS AN ADMINISTRATOR?

In the previous chapter we briefly outlined the steps in the handling of an estate where the deceased left a will. Some differences obviously exist where the deceased died intestate (i.e., without leaving a valid will). This chapter will deal with the application that is made to the court for a Certificate of Appointment of Estate Trustee Without a Will as well as with the fashion in which the estate will be distributed. The estate trustee without a will was formerly known as an administrator.

As in the case of the previous discussion in chapter 3, this chapter is not intended to be an exhaustive study. If you are considering administering the estate of someone who died without a will, it is suggested that *Probate Guide for Ontario* be reviewed for more specific information and examples of forms.

The application to the court is necessary in order to have an estate trustee appointed by the court to administer the estate. In the case where a will is left, that appointment has generally already been made in the will. Obviously, without a will, no such appointment exists.

The general rule is that the closest relative to the deceased has the right to be appointed administrator with the result that if more than one person applies to the court, the nearest relative will generally be appointed as estate trustee.

Although the ultimate decision as to the appointment of an administrator lies with the court, the following order of priority is generally followed:

(a) Spouse of deceased

(b) Children of deceased

(c) Grandchildren of deceased

(d) Parents of deceased

(e) Brothers or sisters of deceased

(f) Nephews or nieces of deceased

Sometimes a person with superior or equal right to apply chooses not to do so and prefers to allow another individual to become the estate trustee. An example of this would be the son of the deceased applying when the deceased had been survived by a widow and two sons. In that situation, two forms known as Renunciation of Prior Right to Certificate of Appointment of Estate Trustee Without a Will and Consent to an Applicant's Appointment as Estate Trustee Without a Will must be completed by both the widow and the other son in order to complete the application.

It should also be noted that a creditor of the estate may apply to be appointed administrator where none of the relatives apply.

If no one applies to be appointed estate trustee, a legal officer known as the public guardian and trustee has the right to become the estate trustee under provincial law. An estate trustee may also be called a personal representative.

b. HOW TO APPLY TO BE AN ESTATE TRUSTEE WITHOUT A WILL

The procedure for obtaining a Certificate of Appointment of Estate Trustee Without a Will is similar to that outlined in the previous chapter. Again, no personal court appearance is necessary. The necessary forms can be purchased from any legal stationer or from the publisher. The forms necessary are not illustrated here, but they are discussed briefly. Examples of the forms can be found in *Probate Guide for Ontario*.

1. Notice of Application for Certificate of Appointment and Affidavit of Service of Notice

This is the same form described in chapter 3 except that it refers to your Application for Appointment as Estate Trustee Without a Will. As explained in chapter 3, it is necessary to send a Notice of your Application to all persons who are entitled to share in the distribution of the estate. Since there is no will, it obviously is not attached to the Notice, and it is not mentioned in the Affidavit of Service of Notice. The Affidavit of Service of Notice is signed in the presence of a notary public, and filed with the other documents.

2. Application for Certificate of Appointment of Estate Trustee Without a Will

This form is similar to the Application illustrated in the last chapter. The main difference is that it sets out the names and addresses of those who will be sharing in the estate. It also contains a statement explaining the applicant's entitlement to the appointment. For instance, the applicant will state that he is the brother of the deceased, or the son, or whatever the case may be. From this statement and the list of those who will share in the estate, the court can assure itself that the applicant is the proper person to apply.

3. Certificate of Appointment of Estate Trustee Without a Will

This is the document which appoints the applicant as estate trustee and authorizes him or her to deal with the assets of the estate. It is prepared by the applicant and submitted to the court to be signed and sealed by the Registrar.

4. Administration Bond

As a general rule, when you apply to be appointed as estate trustee of the estate of a person dying intestate, you must post a bond with the court to ensure that you properly carry out your duties. The bond is generally issued by a bonding company for a premium, much like an insurance policy. Although there is provision in the provincial law for a judge to order that in any particular estate no bond need be filed, obtaining such an order is not always possible, especially if infants are involved. If, however, all of the next-of-kin are over the age of 18 years, it is possible, on proper application, to have the court order that the bond be dispensed with.

The Estates Act also provides that no bond is necessary where the applicant is the surviving spouse of the deceased and where the net value of the estate does not exceed $75 000.

Once all documents are prepared and signed, one copy of each is filed with the court for the county or region in which the deceased resided prior to death. The court fees are $5 for every $1 000, or part thereof, of estate assets up to $50 000, and $15 for every $1 000 of estate assets over $50 000. (As mentioned in chapter 3, these fees have been declared unconstitutional by the Supreme Court of Canada.) Within a week or so (depending on how busy the particular court is), the Certificate will be issued from the court appointing the applicant as estate trustee and putting him or her in a position to be able to deal with the assets of the estate.

Once the Certificate of Appointment of Estate Trustee has been issued, the balance of the administration of the estate is virtually identical to the administration of an estate where the deceased died testate. The major difference is, of course, that there is no will to determine how the estate is to be distributed. Provincial law determines this distribution.

c. HOW IS THE ESTATE DIVIDED IF THERE IS NO WILL?

The Succession Law Reform Act dictates the distribution of an estate on an intestacy. It would probably be worthwhile to obtain a legal opinion about the division of the estate even if you propose to do the administration work without the aid of a lawyer. Anyone distributing an estate improperly is open to a suit by any beneficiary or heir who gets less than the proper share. In other words, a personal representative is personally liable for mistakes made in the distribution of the assets.

I mention again that legitimate and illegitimate relatives rank equally on an intestacy. The personal representative is required by law to make "reasonable enquiries for persons who may be entitled by virtue of a relationship traced through a birth outside marriage." If the personal representative should fail to make reasonable enquiries and if an illegitimate relative exists who should have been included in the distribution, the personal representative can be held personally liable for the loss.

The statute does not say what "reasonable enquiries" are. It is obvious that the personal administrator will have to ask all family members the potentially embarrassing question. Friends, business associates, as well as the deceased's lawyer and doctor should also be asked. It would undoubtedly be a good idea to make the enquiry in writing and to get the responses in written form.

In addition to questioning the deceased's friends and relatives, the personal representative should also search the records of parentage at the office of the Registrar General of Ontario. This office maintains an index of fathers who complete a declaration of paternity when a child is born or who were the subject of a finding of paternity by a court.

As long as such reasonable enquiries are made, there will be no personal liability on the personal representative even if an illegitimate heir turns up after the estate has been distributed. This rule is not limited to illegitimate children only; it applies to any illegitimate heir.

Part II of the Succession Law Reform Act gives no recognition to the common-law spouse although it recognizes the children of such a common-law relationship. The only rights that a common-law spouse has under the legislation is in Part V of the act dealing with support obligations of a deceased. These are discussed in the next chapter.

The rules that follow are to be applied in all cases where the deceased died without a will.

1. A married person with issue

The rules that govern distribution to surviving widows and widowers are under Part II of the Succession Law Reform Act.

(a) The surviving spouse can take the first $200 000 of the net value of the estate. In addition, where there is one child, the surviving spouse will also take one-half of the residue (i.e., the amount in excess of $200 000) and the child will take the other half of the residue. If more than one child is living, the surviving spouse will take one-third of the excess over $200 000 and the remaining two-thirds will be divided equally among the children.

(b) If some but not all of the children die before the intestate, the children of the deceased children (i.e., the grandchildren of the intestate) will share equally the share to which the deceased child (their parent) would have been entitled if living. In such circumstances the number of shares created is determined by the number of children (whether now living or dead) that the deceased had, but the children who died before the intestate are counted only if they, in turn, had children who survived the intestate.

(c) If all of the children of the intestate have died before the deceased, but there are grandchildren living, the portion of the estate that does not pass to a surviving spouse is divided equally among the grandchildren who are alive when the intestate died no matter how many children the deceased had.

The law relating to representation by children of deceased issue can be complex. You are urged to seek legal counsel before attempting to distribute the assets of an estate in this situation.

2. A person with issue but no spouse

(a) If someone dies leaving no surviving spouse, but leaving one child, the whole of the estate will pass to the one surviving child.

(b) If two or more children survive, the entire estate is divided equally among the surviving children.

(c) If some but not all of the children of the deceased die before the parent, the children of the deceased child (i.e., the grandchildren of the intestate) will share equally the share to which the deceased child (their parent) would have been entitled if living. In these circumstances, the number of shares into which the estate is divided is determined by the number of children (whether living or dead) that the deceased had, but the children who died before the intestate are counted only if they, in turn, had children who survived the intestate.

(d) If all of the children of the intestate die before him or her, but there are grandchildren living, the estate is divided equally among the grandchildren living when the intestate died, without reference to the number of children that the deceased had.

Again, you are warned of the complexities involved when representation of deceased heirs is involved.

3. A spouse without issue

Under the Succession Law Reform Act if there are no issue alive at the time of the death of the intestate, the surviving spouse is entitled to the whole estate.

4. A person with no spouse and no issue

The Succession Law Reform Act creates a scheme of distribution similar to the class structure of the former legislation. For convenience we continue to refer to these as classes. The first five classes are as follows:

Class One: Father, mother
Class Two: Brothers, sisters
Class Three: Nephews, nieces
Class Four: Grandmother, grandfather
Class Five: Uncles, aunts

As long as there is at least one next-of-kin living in the closest class, that single individual will inherit the whole estate. No other next-of-kin in a more distant class, regardless of the number that may exist, will receive any benefits under Part II of the Succession Law Reform Act.

For example, if the deceased left no wife or issue and was survived by his mother (his father having predeceased him), the whole estate would pass to the mother regardless of whether there were any other living relatives in any of the other classes.

The rule of representation continues to affect the straightforward rules outlined above. The rule affects the situation where brothers and sisters are inheriting and some but not all of the brothers and sisters have died before the intestate and left children. The children of a deceased sibling share the portion of the estate that their parent would have inherited if alive.

d. DISTRIBUTION OF ESTATE WITHIN A YEAR

Provincial law prohibits an estate trustee without a will from distributing the assets of the estate to the beneficiaries within one year of the death of the deceased unless he or she advertised for creditors. This is a very important restriction on the power of the estate trustee. No such limitation applies to an estate trustee with a will.

Except as stated above, there is never any obligation on an estate trustee to advertise for creditors. It is, however, a wise precaution in most estate situations to do so. (See chapter 3 for an example of the necessary advertisement for creditors.)

5
TESTAMENTARY FREEDOM

Traditionally, under Anglo-Canadian law, a testator was permitted unfettered discretion when it came to the disposition of the assets by will. This concept is referred to as "testamentary freedom." This principle of law has been eroded over the years by various legislative enactments of our provincial government. For example, prior to these enactments, if a testator with an estate valued at $500 000 chose to leave everything to his mistress and nothing to his wife, he was able to do so.

Over the years, it was recognized that this type of situation was undesirable and, consequently, legislative limitations on testamentary freedom have been imposed. This chapter explores two significant pieces of such legislation: the Succession Law Reform Act, which has been in force in Ontario since March 31, 1978; and the Family Law Act, 1986, which was enacted by the provincial legislature and proclaimed in force in early 1986.

a. THE SUCCESSION LAW REFORM ACT

Reference has previously been made to the enactment of the Succession Law Reform Act, which came into effect in Ontario on March 31, 1978. Part V of that act imposes certain support obligations that come into effect on the death of an individual. Generally speaking, Part V imposes an obligation of support in favor of a group of individuals known as "dependants" of the deceased person. The act defines a dependant as the spouse or common-law spouse of the deceased, a parent or grandparent of the deceased, a child or grandchild of the deceased, or a brother or sister of the deceased, provided that the deceased was providing support or was under a legal obligation to provide support immediately before his or her death to any such person. Children include not only natural children, but anyone whom the deceased has demonstrated a settled intention to treat as a child of his or her family.

The act defines common-law spouses as persons who, although not married to each other, had been cohabiting immediately before the death of one of them for a continuous period of not less than three years or, alternatively, in a relationship of some permanence where there is a child born of whom they are the natural parents. As well, the act defines a spouse to include a former spouse. Accordingly, the definition of dependant includes a person from whom the deceased was divorced.

In order to be a dependant, two tests must be met. First, the person must fall within the group of individuals outlined above. Second, the person must have been receiving support or must have been legally entitled to support immediately before the death of the deceased. It is not enough that an individual claiming support be the child of the deceased. He or she must also establish that the deceased was providing support or was obliged to supply support to him or her immediately prior to the death of the deceased.

It is from Part V of the Succession Law Reform Act that a common-law spouse now gets some protection that he or she did not have prior to March 31, 1978. Although the common-law spouse is still not recognized as a spouse for the purposes of a distribution on an intestacy, Part V of the Succession Law Reform Act does allow a common-law spouse (if he or she meets the tests outlined above) to make a claim as a dependant of the deceased whether the deceased left a will or not.

The inclusion of a former spouse as a "dependant" is quite a dramatic change in what had previously been recognized as support obligations. If the deceased was providing support or was under a legal obligation to provide support to a divorced spouse immediately before death, the former spouse qualifies as a dependant. Since many separation agreements and court orders given at the time of divorce customarily place an obligation on one spouse to pay support or maintenance payments to the other, a former spouse will, in those instances, qualify as a dependant.

The act goes further to define a child to include a grandchild and "a person whom the deceased demonstrated a settled intention to treat as a child of his family." This latter definition qualifies a person as a dependant who is not even related to the deceased person, but to whom the deceased was giving support and was treating as his or her own child.

As indicated earlier, support obligations contained in the Succession Law Reform Act can be invoked by a dependant whether there is a will or not. Thus it is possible, for example, for the son of a deceased person to be entitled to a certain share of his father's estate on an intestacy and yet to bring an application as a dependant based on the argument that the share is not enough and that he should be awarded more from the balance of the estate. Obviously, if such an award is made to any dependant, the effect is that some other person's share of the estate will be reduced.

Once an individual is recognized as a dependant, Part V of the Succession Law Reform Act goes on to provide that application can be made to the court for an order that support for such dependant be paid out of the estate of the deceased. The dependant, in this situation, must establish to the court that the deceased, whether testate or intestate, has not made "adequate provision for the proper support" of such dependant. It is not enough for an applicant to merely qualify as a dependant; the applicant must also establish that there is financial need.

Section 62 of the Succession Law Reform Act sets out a lengthy list of the matters that a court is to consider when determining if and how much of an allowance should be made to a dependant from the estate of the deceased. These include such obvious factors as —

(a) the assets and means of the dependant,

(b) the capacity of the dependant to provide for his or her own support,

(c) the age and physical and mental health of the dependant,

(d) the needs of the dependant, in determining which the court may consider the accustomed standard of living of such person,

(e) the proximity and duration of the dependant's relationship with the deceased,

(f) the contributions made by the dependant to the deceased's welfare, including indirect and nonfinancial contributions,

(g) the contributions made by the dependant to the acquisition, maintenance, and improvement of the deceased's property, business, or occupation,

(h) whether the dependant has a legal obligation to provide support for another person,

(i) when the dependant is a child, his or her aptitude for and reasonable prospects of obtaining an education, and

(j) where the dependant is a child of the age of 16 years or more, his or her withdrawal from parental control.

The legislation has not attempted to define "adequate provision for the proper support" of a dependant. Rather, it has given the court guidelines, so a considerable amount of discretion lies with the judge hearing any application. It is virtually impossible to predict with any certainty the amount that any court would order as an allowance to a successful applicant. Even though there are a multitude of decided cases relating to support obligations, each case is different and will be decided on its own facts.

Applications under Part V of the Succession Law Reform Act are made to the Ontario Court (General Division) of the county or region in which the deceased lived at the time of death. Thus, if the deceased person did not live in Ontario at the time of his or her death, no application by a dependant is possible under the Succession Law Reform Act even if the dependant lives in Ontario. Most of the other provinces and many other countries have similar (but not identical) legislation. If the deceased person lived in Manitoba at the time of death, for example, the dependant would then be governed by Manitoba legislation rather than by the Succession Law Reform Act and would have to seek remedies in that province.

Under Part V of the act, an application must be made by a dependant within six months from the grant of a Certificate of Appointment of Estate Trustee. An extension of this period may be allowed by the court if it considers it proper. However, in the case of a successful late application, any award will only affect the portion of the estate of the deceased that remains undistributed at the date of application. Accordingly, if an application is granted after one year following the grant of Certificate of Appointment of Estate Trustee and if, by that date, the whole of the estate has been paid out to those named in the will, no order will be made despite a person establishing that he or she is a dependant.

1. What dependants might receive

If the court grants an application by a dependant, Part V of the Succession Law Reform Act provides for a broad range of possible orders. The court may order the estate to make periodic (such as annual or monthly) payments to the dependant for an indefinite period or for a specified number of years, or until the happening of a certain event. It is possible, for example, that an order could be made for monthly payments to a spouse or common-law spouse until he or she remarried. Or, to take another example, an order could be made for payments to a dependant in school until he or she graduated or left university.

A lump sum payment is also contemplated by the act. As well, the court may order a specific asset or article to be transferred to a dependant. The legislation also contemplates an order that would permit a dependant possession or use of any specified property for the balance of the lifetime of such dependant or for such period as the court considers appropriate.

In order to secure any payment under an order made under Part V, the court may place a charge (similar to a mortgage) on any other property of the estate. Note that the court has an extremely wide discretion as to the type of order that can be made. The most common type of order has traditionally been the periodic payments, although lump sum awards are made where periodic payments would unduly delay the winding up and distribution of an estate.

The Succession Law Reform Act also provides for a re-hearing at a subsequent date, permitting the court to vary, discharge, suspend, or enquire into the adequacy of any order previously made. Thus, if after an award is made, the fortunes of a dependant improve, a further application could be brought by the beneficiaries of the estate (out of whose share the award was made) to have the payments reduced or even terminated. Similarly, if a dependant falls upon hard times and is able to convince the court that he or she should receive a larger amount from the estate, the court has the ability to order larger payments.

The support obligations imposed by Part V of the Succession Law Reform Act also affect assets that, strictly speaking, do not form part of a deceased's estate. As described earlier, jointly held assets and life insurance proceeds payable to a named beneficiary are not estate assets. Notwithstanding this fact, Section 72 of the Succession Law Reform Act provides that, in certain circumstances, jointly held property and proceeds of life insurance policies are to be considered as part of the value of the estate of the deceased person when considering an application by a dependant under Part V. A life insurance policy can be protected from such inclusion by having the policy owned by someone else.

For example, a man living in a common-law relationship might have his common-law wife apply for insurance on his life (with the proceeds payable to her in the event of death) rather than having the man, himself, purchase the insurance policy. This mere difference in ownership of the policy would protect proceeds from attack by a dependant of the common-law husband in the event of his death and would ensure that no order could be made under Part V which would affect the proceeds of that policy. It is theoretically possible for a deceased's ex-wife, present wife (from whom he is separated), and common-law wife to all simultaneously apply to the court as dependants.

2. Consider legal advice

As you can see, it is very important to keep the provisions of Part V of the Succession Law Reform Act in mind when making your will. Although the legislation does not require a testator to include provisions in the will for dependants, if he or she fails to do so, an application can be made after death by a dependant that could alter the dispositions. If you propose to exclude from your will someone who qualifies as a dependant, and who might bring a successful application after your death, it is recommended that you seek legal advice before doing so. Similarly, if you are a dependant, and feel that you are entitled to make a claim against the estate of a deceased, you should seek legal advice.

This outline of a rather extensive area of the law is intended to inform you of your support rights and support obligations under Part V of the Succession Law Reform Act. This area of the law is quite complex, however, and you should not get too deeply involved in it without legal assistance.

b. THE FAMILY LAW ACT, 1986

The second piece of legislation limiting testamentary freedom is known as the Family Law Act, 1986.

1. The concept of "net family property"

Generally, and subject to the exceptions listed below, the "net family property" of a married person at the time of his or her death is the value of all of the property of that person at the date of death less debts and liabilities. A number of assets are, however, excluded when calculating a person's net family property. These exceptions are as follows:

(a) The value of property, other than a matrimonial home, that was owned by the deceased on the date of marriage, after deducting the deceased's debts and other liabilities at the date of the marriage

(b) The value of all property, other than a matrimonial home, that was acquired by gift or inheritance from a third person after the date of marriage

(c) Any income arising from a gift or inheritance where the person making the gift or leaving the inheritance has expressly stated that it is to be excluded from the recipient's net family property

(d) Certain types of damage awards made by a court for personal injuries, nervous shock, mental distress, and similar causes of action

(e) Proceeds or a right to proceeds of a life insurance policy

(f) Property, other than a matrimonial home, into which any of the property described in sub-paragraphs (b) to (e) above can be traced

(g) Property that the deceased and his or her spouse had previously agreed, in the form of a contract between them, would not be included in the spouse's net family property.

The application of this formula will result in the determination of a dollar amount as the net family property of the deceased person. It is obvious that in many instances it will be very difficult to calculate net family property especially where spouses have been married for an extended period of time. Nevertheless, the value of the net family property of a deceased person will have to be calculated in many instances in connection with the distribution of the estate.

It may also be necessary to calculate the net family property of the surviving spouse.

2. Entitlement of surviving spouse

Section 5(2) of the Family Law Act provides that, where a married person dies, if the net family property of the deceased person exceeds the net family property of the surviving spouse, the surviving spouse is entitled to one-half of the difference. For example, assume a wealthy man dies with a net family property, when calculated at the time of his death, of $2 000 000. Assume also that the calculation of his surviving wife's net family property results in a value of $100 000. The effect of the legislation is that, irrespective of any provisions in the will of the deceased, the widow is entitled to one-half of the difference between the two net family property values, such entitlement being $950 000.

The calculation of net family property is carried out as of the day immediately prior to the date on which the deceased spouse dies, leaving the other spouse surviving.

The Family Law Act does, however, contain a provision that gives the court a discretion to vary the rigid effect of Section 5(2) described above. Briefly, the court is given the power to award a spouse more or less than one-half the difference between the net family properties if the court is of the opinion that equalizing the net family properties would be "unconscionable" after considering certain matters spelled out in the act, including —

(a) a spouse's failure to disclose to the other spouse debts or liabilities existing at the date of marriage,

(b) the fact that debts or other liabilities claimed in reduction of a spouse's net family property were incurred recklessly or in bad faith,

(c) gifts made by one spouse to another during marriage,

(d) a spouse's intentional or reckless depletion of his or her net family property,

(e) the fact that the amount a spouse would otherwise receive under the legislation is disproportionately large in relation to a period of cohabitation that is less than five years,

(f) the fact that one spouse has incurred a disproportionately larger amount of debts or other liabilities than the other spouse for the support of the family,

(g) a written agreement between the spouses, and

(h) any other circumstances the court deems to be relevant.

There is a great deal of scope and discretion given to the court to disregard the rigid division of net family property that would result from applying Section 5(2) of the act.

3. Elections to be made by surviving spouse

Section 6(1) of the Family Law Act, clearly states that when a spouse dies leaving a will, the surviving spouse must elect to take under the will or to receive the entitlement under Section 5 described above of the Family Law Act. Where a spouse dies without a will, the surviving spouse must elect to receive the entitlement under Part II of the Succession Law Reform

Act or to receive the entitlement under Section 5 of the Family Law Act, 1985. (Provisions of Part II of the Succession Law Reform Act are discussed in chapter 4.)

There is a provision in the Family Law Act that allows the surviving spouse to receive both the gifts made to him or her in the deceased spouse's will and the entitlement under Section 5 of the Family Law Act if the will in question expressly provides for that result. Accordingly, it is possible to include such a provision in a will.

The election referred to above must be made in writing by the surviving spouse and filed in the court clerk's office within six months after the first spouse's death. The act provides that if a surviving spouse does not file an election within that time period, he or she shall be deemed to have elected to take under the will or to receive entitlement under the Succession Law Reform Act. Accordingly, the provisions of the Family Law Act will only protect a surviving spouse if he or she elects to take the entitlement under the act within six months of the death of his or her spouse.

4. Restrictions on distribution of estate

As a consequence of the time period for filing an election by the surviving spouse, the Family Law Act prohibits the distribution of the estate of the deceased spouse within six months of death unless the surviving spouse gives written consent to distribution or the court authorizes such distribution. Furthermore, no distribution shall be made in the administration of any estate after the executor or administrator has received notice of an application under the Family Law Act, unless the applicant gives written consent to the distribution or the court authorizes the distribution.

5. Comments

In the simple situation of a husband and wife who have no matrimonial difficulties and whose assets are not substantial, undoubtedly the provisions of the Family Law Act will never come into play. Obviously, where a surviving spouse is left everything under the will of his or her deceased spouse, the legislation has no relevance. However, it can readily be seen that the legislation will have a dramatic effect in situations where a deceased person attempts to exclude the surviving spouse from sharing equally in the family property. The effect of the legislation could result in substantial interference with the provisions of such a deceased person's will. One way to prevent this interference is for the testator or testatrix to enter into a written marriage contract with his or her spouse in which all claims against the estate of the other are released. For a detailed discussion of marriage contracts, see *Marriage, Separation, and Divorce*, another title in the Self-Counsel Series.

6

TAXES

a. SUCCESSION DUTY

The Succession Duty Act, a statute of the province of Ontario, was originally enacted in 1930. The act imposed a death tax on any property situated in the province that passed to an heir, beneficiary, or next-of-kin on the death of a person.

The act also taxed certain property situated outside of Ontario if the deceased person was domiciled (i.e., made his or her permanent home) in Ontario at the time of death. Although the legislation is somewhat complex, generally speaking it taxed the whole estate of an Ontario resident upon his or her death.

In 1979, Ontario enacted legislation which provides that the Succession Duty Act does not apply to any death occurring after April 10, 1979. The legislation has not been repealed. It continues in full force and effect, and it imposes a provincial death tax on estates where the deceased died on or before April 10, 1979.

If you are involved in an estate where the deceased died on or before April 10, 1979, you are urged to obtain legal assistance.

Where a person has died after April 10, 1979, the Succession Duty Act can be completely ignored. The act has no application, and there are no provincial death duties to be concerned about.

b. FOREIGN DEATH DUTIES

If the deceased person did not live permanently in Ontario or lived in Ontario, but owned assets outside of Ontario, the personal representative may be required to file death tax returns elsewhere. At the time of writing, Quebec still imposes a succession duty similar (though not identical) to that formerly imposed by Ontario. Likewise many foreign countries and states impose death taxes of their own, some similar to that previously imposed by the province of Ontario and some radically different. If the deceased owned a ski chalet in Quebec and real property in Florida while living in Ontario, the personal representative would have to file a Quebec Succession Duty Return and a Florida death tax return.

Since the laws and the basis of the tax differ from province to province and from state to state, the services of experienced legal counsel in these other jurisdictions may be necessary.

c. CAPITAL GAINS TAX

A capital gains tax is a tax based on the amount of profit or gain made by a person when he or she disposes of an asset. For example, if Gordon buys 10 shares of Bell Canada in July, 1994, for $420 (including brokerage charges) and sells those 10 shares in October, 1997, for $460 (after deducting brokerage charges), he has a capital gain of $40.

All taxpayers must declare the gain on the tax return filed for the year in which the property is sold. Under current law, three-quarters of all capital gains are added to other income of the taxpayer and taxed. If Gordon were an employee making $14 000 salary, $30, which is three-quarters of his capital gain, would be added to the income. From this total of $14 030, deductions would be made and tax calculated.

Had Gordon sold the shares of Bell Canada at a $20 loss, it would be called a capital loss, the reverse of a capital gain. In this situation, three-quarters of the capital loss (or $15) would be deducted from his other income when calculating his income tax for the year. There are limits upon the total amount of capital losses which may be deducted in any one year.

Though a capital gain is normally only experienced and taxed when an asset is sold or given away, the Income Tax Act provides for the imposition of this tax when the individual dies. This is referred to as a "deemed disposition."

d. HOW TO FILE THE DECEASED'S INCOME TAX RETURN

One of the many duties of the personal representative is to file the income tax return for the deceased person for the year of death, along with any other returns not yet filed.

The personal representative is allowed six months or until April 30, whichever is the longer period, to file the income tax return for the year of death.

Say, for example, Thomas Taxed died on March 1, 1997. At that time Mr. Taxed had probably not yet filed his 1996 income tax return which was not due until April 30, 1997. His personal representative would have to file the deceased's tax return for the 1996 taxation year by September 1, 1997, and to file the deceased's 1997 tax return (for the part of the year during which he was alive) by April 30, 1998.

In preparing and filing the deceased's income tax return, the personal representative must declare gains on all the assets owned by the deceased on the day of death as though the deceased had sold all assets on that date. Any increase in value over the cost of the assets in the estate will result in a capital gain, three-quarters of which is taxable.

The Income Tax Act provides specifically for an exemption from capital gains tax on death if the property upon which a capital gain has been realized passes to the spouse of the deceased person either under provisions of a will or on an intestacy. Thus, no capital gains tax is due on any property which Jane Ellen Smith's husband inherits on her death. But if she leaves property to a sister, for example, the personal representative must obtain values for it and calculate the capital gains or losses.

e. VALUATION DAYS

For any property acquired after December, 1971, the capital gain is measured simply by deducting the actual cost from the value of the property on the date of death. However, in drafting the provisions of the Income Tax Act, it was decided that it would be unfair to tax any capital gains made before the law came into effect. Hence, only increases in value which have accrued since January 1, 1972 are subject to a capital gains tax.

In order to measure any capital gain on property acquired before the new tax system began, but sold or deemed to be disposed of because of death after December 31, 1971, the value of the property just before the new tax system began must be determined. This value will generally be deducted from value at the date of death to determine the capital gain. The federal government designated two "valuation days" for the valuing of property immediately prior to the beginning of the new tax system. December 22, 1971, is valuation day for publicly traded stocks and shares, while December 31, 1971, is valuation day for all other property. For property acquired before December, 1971, capital gains or losses are calculated based on the value of the property on valuation day, not the cost of the property when acquired.

For example, if Frank Farmer acquired 100 acres of vacant land in Muskoka for $1 000 in 1950 and it was appraised at $95 000 on his death in 1995, the capital gain is not measured as $94 000 ($95 000 minus $1 000). Rather, it is necessary for the personal representative to find the value of the acreage as of the valuation day, December 31, 1971. Assume that this value amounted to $80 000. The capital gain for tax purposes is then only $15 000 ($95 000 minus $80 000), three-quarters of which is subject to tax.

Needless to say, the above examples over-simplify the procedure and calculations. There are special rules which apply in situations where property has fluctuated in value over the years rather than simply increasing or decreasing in value in a straight line. The rules are complex. Only in rare circumstances should you attempt to carry through such calculation without legal assistance.

7

THE CANADA PENSION PLAN

a. BENEFITS UNDER THE PLAN

Too often people forget Canada Pension Plan benefits which are payable on the death of a deceased contributor. Practically all individuals earning income from employment as well as self-employed individuals must contribute to the plan.

On the death of any individual who has contributed to the plan during the minimum qualifying period, three possible types of survivor's benefits are available:

(a) A lump-sum death benefit payable to the estate or to the surviving spouse to help offset funeral expenses

(b) A monthly pension to the surviving spouse (husband or wife), if any

(c) A monthly pension for dependent children, if any

Generally speaking, the act defines the minimum qualifying period as one-third of the calendar years for which the person (deceased) was required to contribute to the plan or ten calendar years, whichever is less. In no case can the minimum be less than three years.

The personal representative and the surviving spouse should carefully consider the potential benefits to see which, if any, are payable in the particular circumstances of the estate with which they are dealing.

b. LUMP-SUM DEATH BENEFIT

A lump-sum death benefit is payable to the estate of a person who contributed to the plan for the minimum qualifying period. A person is required to contribute to the plan from January 1, 1966 or from the month following his or her 18th birthday, whichever occurs later. The application for the lump-sum death benefit is made by the personal representative.

The size of the lump-sum payment will depend on the amount actually contributed to the plan by the deceased. The amount is calculated on the basis of six times the monthly retirement pension that he or she was collecting. If the deceased was not yet collecting a pension, then a calculation is made to see what the pension would have been at the date of death if he or she had been eligible for a pension on that date. The lump-sum amount will be six times the hypothetical pension. The maximum lump-sum death benefit payment for a death which occurred in 1997 is $3 580.

Application forms for the lump-sum death benefit can be obtained free of charge upon request at any office of the Canada Pension Plan. Various documents must accompany the application. These include —

(a) a death certificate,

(b) deceased's birth certificate,

(c) deceased's social insurance card.

An Application for Death Benefit is shown in Sample #14.

The death benefit is the only benefit that is retroactive for more than one year. So, even if the executors or administrators of an estate overlooked this benefit five years ago, they could put in an application today.

c. SURVIVOR'S PENSION

If the deceased contributor is survived by a spouse, whether male or female, he or she may be eligible for a survivor's pension. It is once again necessary for the deceased person to have contributed to the plan for the minimum contributory period. The precise amount of the monthly pension depends on a number of factors including the amount of actual contributions to the plan, the age of the applicant, and the number of dependent children who survive the deceased.

Under the Canada Pension Plan, no survivor's pension is payable to a person who was, at the time of the death of the contributor, under the age of 35, unless that person has dependent children or is disabled or subsequently becomes disabled.

Application forms for the survivor's pension can be obtained free of charge from any office of the Canada Pension Plan. (See Sample #15.)

Various documents must accompany the application. These include —

(a) a death certificate or funeral director's statement of death,

(b) deceased's birth certificate,

(c) deceased's social insurance card,

(d) the marriage certificate,

(e) survivor's birth certificate,

(f) survivor's social insurance card.

Four of the required documents duplicate the requirements for the application for a lump-sum death benefit. If both types of benefits are being applied for, it is usual to send in both applications at the same time.

The plan includes regulations regarding the entitlement to a survivor's pension in situations where the spouse remarries or where the husband and wife separated or were divorced prior to the death.

For the purpose of receiving a survivor's pension, the surviving spouse can be a legal or a common-law spouse. A common-law spouse is defined as a person who lived in a conjugal relationship with the deceased for at least one year prior to the date of death.

A separated legal spouse is eligible for a survivor's pension, except where an eligible common-law spouse applies for the benefit.

A spouse who is divorced from a deceased contributor is not eligible for a pension at all.

d. BENEFITS FOR DEPENDENT CHILDREN

Benefits for dependent children are also payable on the death of a contributor. To be eligible for the benefits payable, the child must be unmarried, the natural or adopted child of the deceased contributor, and under the age of 18 or between 18 and 25 if the child attends school or university full-time.

The result of a successful application will be a monthly pension payable to the parent or guardian of the child until he or she is 18. If the pension continues after the age of 18 because the child is in full-time attendance at school or university, it is payable directly to the child. The child's pension continues only as long as he or she meets the qualifications for eligibility stated above.

The application form for a survivor's pension doubles as an application for benefits for dependent children under the age of 18. By filling in additional parts of the form, the two applications are made simultaneously. If application is being made by a child over the age of 18, a separate form is available from the local office of the Canada Pension Plan.

Additional documents that will be required include —

(a) the birth certificate of each child, and

(b) a social insurance card (if any) for each child.

SAMPLE #14
APPLICATION FOR DEATH BENEFIT

Health and Welfare Canada
Income Security Programs

Santé et Bien-être social Canada
Programmes de la sécurité du revenu

Français au verso
Personal Information
Bank NHW/P-PU-147
FOR PERTINENT INFORMATION WITH RESPECT TO THE PRIVACY ACT, PLEASE SEE INFORMATION SHEET.

APPLICATION
DEATH BENEFIT
CANADA PENSION PLAN

COMPLETE THE UNSHADED AREAS
PLEASE PRINT

LANGUAGE PREFERENCE
ENGLISH ☒ FRENCH ☐

SECTION A — INFORMATION ABOUT THE DECEASED CONTRIBUTOR

FOR OFFICE USE ONLY

1A. CONTRIBUTOR'S SOCIAL INSURANCE NUMBER	1B. Male ☒ Female ☐	1C. DATE OF BIRTH Day Month Year	AGE ESTABLISHED
9 8 7 6 5 4 3 2 1		2 1 1 1 4 3	AA

2A. MARITAL STATUS: Single ☐ Married ☒ Separated ☐ Widow(er) ☐ Divorced ☐ Common-law ☐

2B. DATE OF DEATH Day Month Year 0 1 1 0 3 9 1

DATE OF DEATH ESTABL | PROV. CODE | AA

3. MR., MRS., ETC. GIVEN NAME AND INITIAL: MR. JOHN A.   FAMILY NAME: SMITH

SURNAME — VALIDATOR | AR

4. HOME ADDRESS (Number and Street): 42 ROSE AVENUE,   (Apt. No., P.O. Box, R.R. No.)

5. (City, Town or Village) TORONTO, (Province or Territory) ONTARIO (Country) CANADA (Postal Code) M 7 Y 2 B 2

6A. IF ADDRESS ABOVE IS OUTSIDE OF CANADA, INDICATE THE PROVINCE IN WHICH THE DECEASED LAST RESIDED.

6B. DECEASED'S LAST NAME AT BIRTH Same as 3. ☐ or above ☒

7A. WAS THE DECEASED EVER IN RECEIPT OF, OR HAD THE DECEASED EVER APPLIED FOR A BENEFIT UNDER: The Canada Pension Plan? Yes ☐ No ☒ The Quebec Pension Plan? Yes ☐ No ☒ The Old Age Security Act? Yes ☐ No ☒

7B. IF YES, INDICATE UNDER WHAT SOCIAL INSURANCE NUMBER.

8. HAS THE DECEASED EVER PARTICIPATED IN A SOCIAL INSURANCE PLAN OF ANOTHER COUNTRY? Yes ☐ No ☒   INDICATE NAME OF COUNTRY(IES) AND INSURANCE NUMBER(S).

9A. IF APPLICABLE, INDICATE SPOUSE'S FULL NAME AND SOCIAL INSURANCE NUMBER, IF AVAILABLE.
MARY M. SMITH   9 8 6 6 5 3 3 2 0

9B. IS THERE: Yes No
AN EXECUTOR OF THE ESTATE? ☒ ☐
OR AN ADMINISTRATOR OF THE ESTATE? ☐ ☐
OR A LEGAL REPRESENTATIVE OF THE ESTATE? ☐ ☐ | A

10. THE ESTATE OF JOHN A. SMITH

11. INDICATE COMPLETE NAME OF PERSON OR AGENCY AND ITS REPRESENTATIVE REFERRED TO IN QUESTION 9B. (if applicable)
MARY MATILDA SMITH | B

12. ADDRESS OF PERSON OR AGENCY NAMED IN 11. 42 ROSE AVENUE   (Apt. No., P.O. Box, R.R. No.)

TYPE NM ADR | FOREIGN CODE | LANG. | C

13. (City, Town or Village) TORONTO, (Province or Territory) ONTARIO (Country) CANADA (Postal Code) M 7 Y 2 B 2

CONS. CODE | NO. LNS 2 1 0 | D

14. NO THE DECEASED OR THE DECEASED'S SPOUSE RECEIVE FAMILY ALLOWANCES SINCE JANUARY 1, 1966, FOR CHILDREN BORN AFTER DECEMBER 31, 1958?
DECEASED CONTRIBUTOR Yes ☐ DECEASED'S SPOUSE No ☒ Yes ☐

SECTION B — INFORMATION ABOUT THE APPLICANT

15A. MR., MRS., ETC. GIVEN NAME AND INITIAL MRS. MARY M.	FAMILY NAME SMITH	15B. RELATIONSHIP OF APPLICANT TO DECEASED WIFE	A

16. FOR THE ESTATE OF JOHN A. SMITH   ADDRESS (Number and Street, Apt. No., P.O. Box, R.R. No.) 42 ROSE AVENUE,

TYPE NM ADR | FOREIGN CODE | LANG. | B

17. (City, Town or Village) TORONTO, (Province or Territory) ONTARIO (Country) CANADA (Postal Code) M 7 Y 2 B 2

CONS. CODE | NO. LNS 2 1 0 | A.L. | C

SECTION C — DECLARATION OF THE APPLICANT

18. I hereby apply on behalf of the estate of the deceased contributor for a Death Benefit. I declare that, to the best of my knowledge and belief, the information given in this application is true and complete.

SIGNATURE OF APPLICANT Mary M. Smith

DATE OF APPLICATION Day Month Year 1 5 0 3 9 1

TELEPHONE NUMBER (416) 222-3333

IT IS AN OFFENCE TO MAKE A FALSE OR MISLEADING STATEMENT IN THIS APPLICATION.

OFFICE USE ONLY — DO NOT WRITE BELOW THIS LINE

BENEFIT INFORMATION ACTION BNFT: D T H 2 0 AL 0 0 B/C D E F G S: 0 0 C.P.P. NUMBER APP. REC'D D M Y DT. EFF. M Y | EA

MONETARY INFO

CODE	CHILD BENE	RECOVERY SHFT CHILD	SIGN	UNDER/OVPYMT	ACCRUED RECOVERY CPP	OPP	DT. EFF. M Y	CPP WITHHOLD ARREARS	RATE	OPP WITHHOLD ARREARS	RATE	
												FA
												FA
												FA
TOTAL			►									FB

EARNINGS

YR	TYPE	PLAN	CATEGORY	EARNINGS	CONTRIBUTIONS	TOTAL EARNINGS	CONTRIBUTIONS	DATE APPLICATION RECEIVED	
									GA
									GB

Application taken by: _____ Date: _____

Application approved pursuant to Subsection 59(3) of the Canada Pension Plan. Authorized Signature: _____

DATE	TYPE OF REJECT	BATCH NO.	CYCLE	DATE	SIGNATURE
1					
2					

ISP 1200 (4-90)

HWC PROTECTED

101

SAMPLE #15
APPLICATION FOR SURVIVORS' BENEFIT

Health and Welfare Canada — Income Security Programs
Santé et Bien-être social Canada — Programmes de la sécurité du revenu

Personal Information
Bank HWW/P-PU-147
FOR PERTINENT INFORMATION WITH RESPECT TO THE PRIVACY ACT, PLEASE SEE INFORMATION SHEET.

APPLICATION
SURVIVORS' BENEFITS
CANADA PENSION PLAN

COMPLETE THE UNSHADED AREAS
PLEASE PRINT

LANGUAGE PREFERENCE
ENGLISH ☐ FRENCH ☐

SECTION A – INFORMATION ABOUT THE DECEASED CONTRIBUTOR | FOR OFFICE USE ONLY

1A. CONTRIBUTOR'S SOCIAL INSURANCE NUMBER: 9 8 7 6 5 4 3 2 1
1B. Male ☒ Female ☐
1C. DATE OF BIRTH (Day Month Year): 21 11 43 — AGE ESTABLISHED | AA

2A. MARITAL STATUS: Single ☐ Married ☒ Separated ☐ Widow(er) ☐ Divorced ☐ Common-law ☐
2B. DATE OF DEATH (Day Month Year): 01 03 91 — DATE OF DEATH ESTABL. PROV. CODE | AA

3. MR. MRS. ETC. GIVEN NAME AND INITIAL: MR. JOHN A. FAMILY NAME: SMITH — SURNAME – VALIDATOR | AR

4. HOME ADDRESS (Number and Street): 42 ROSE AVENUE (Apt. No., P.O. Box, R.R. No)

5. (City, Town or Village): TORONTO (Province or Territory): ONTARIO (Country): CANADA (Postal Code): M7Y2B2

SECTION B – INFORMATION ABOUT THE SURVIVING SPOUSE | FOR OFFICE USE ONLY

6A. YOUR SOCIAL INSURANCE NUMBER: 9 8 6 6 5 3 3 2 1
6B. Male ☐ Female ☒
6C. YOUR DATE OF BIRTH (Day Month Year): 01 02 45 — AGE ESTABLISHED | AS

7. MR. MRS. ETC. GIVEN NAME AND INITIAL: MRS. MARY M. FAMILY NAME: SMITH — DSB START DSB END | AS

8. HOME ADDRESS (Number and Street): 42 ROSE AVENUE (Apt. No., P.O. Box, R.R. No.) — TYPE HM ADR FOREIGN CODE LANG. | B

9. (City, Town or Village): TORONTO (Province or Territory): ONTARIO (Country): CANADA (Postal Code): M7Y2B2 — CONS. CODE NO LNS A.L. 2 1 | C

10. MAILING ADDRESS IF DIFFERENT FROM 8. ABOVE (Number and Street): N/A — TYPE HM ADR FOREIGN CODE LANG. | CB

11. (City, Town or Village): (Province or Territory): (Country): (Postal Code): — CONS. CODE NO LNS A.L. 2 1 | CC

12A. IF ADDRESS SHOWN IN 8. ABOVE IS OUTSIDE OF CANADA, INDICATE THE LAST PROVINCE OF RESIDENCE: N/A
12B. ARE YOU DISABLED? ☐ Yes ☒ No

13A. ARE YOU RECEIVING OR HAVE YOU EVER RECEIVED OR APPLIED FOR A BENEFIT UNDER: The Canada Pension Plan? ☐ Yes ☒ No   The Quebec Pension Plan? ☐ Yes ☒ No   The Old Age Security Act? ☐ Yes ☒ No
13B. IF YES, INDICATE UNDER WHAT SOCIAL INSURANCE NUMBER.

14. YOUR NAME AT BIRTH SAME AS 7. ABOVE ☐ OR: GARDNER — MARRIAGE ESTABLISHED

15A. WERE YOU MARRIED TO THE DECEASED CONTRIBUTOR? Yes ☒ Enter date of marriage ► (Day) 14 (Month) 06 (Year) 1963 (Submit Marriage Certificate)   No ☐ When did you start living together? (Day) (Month) (Year)
15B. WERE YOU STILL MARRIED AT THE TIME OF THE CONTRIBUTOR'S DEATH? ☒ Yes ☐ No
15C. WERE YOU STILL LIVING TOGETHER AT THE TIME OF THE CONTRIBUTOR'S DEATH? ☒ Yes ☐ No

16. IF YOU WERE UNDER 45 YEARS OF AGE AT THE TIME OF THE CONTRIBUTOR'S DEATH, WERE YOU WHOLLY OR SUBSTANTIALLY MAINTAINING:
A. A CHILD OF THE CONTRIBUTOR UNDER 18 YEARS OF AGE WHO WAS NOT IN YOUR CUSTODY AND CONTROL? ☐ Yes ☒ No
B. A DISABLED CHILD OF THE CONTRIBUTOR AGE 18 OR OVER? ☐ Yes ☒ No
C. A CHILD OF THE CONTRIBUTOR AGE 18 TO 25 IN FULL TIME ATTENDANCE AT SCHOOL OR UNIVERSITY? ☐ Yes ☒ No

If yes to any of the above, explain the circumstances on a separate sheet of paper and indicate whether or not the maintenance is continuing.

SECTION C – INFORMATION ABOUT THE CHILDREN WHO ARE UNDER AGE 18 | FOR OFFICE USE ONLY

17A. SOCIAL INSURANCE NUMBER OF CHILD: 1 2 3 4 5 6 7 8 9
17B. Male ☐ Female ☒
17C. DATE OF BIRTH (Day Month Year): 13 01 77 — AGE ESTABLISHED | CANCELLATION M Y REASON | DA

18. GIVEN NAME OF CHILD: JOANNE INITIAL: M FAMILY NAME: SMITH — DPND END M Y DSB START M Y DSB END M Y A.L. | DA

19A. SOCIAL INSURANCE NUMBER OF CHILD: 9 8 7 6 5 4 3 2 1
19B. Male ☒ Female ☐
19C. DATE OF BIRTH (Day Month Year): 17 04 79 — AGE ESTABLISHED | CANCELLATION M Y REASON | DB

20. GIVEN NAME OF CHILD: PETER T. INITIAL: FAMILY NAME: SMITH — DPND END M Y DSB START M Y DSB END M Y A.L. | DB

LIST ADDITIONAL CHILDREN ON A SEPARATE SHEET OF PAPER AND ATTACH TO THIS APPLICATION

21. ARE ALL OF THE CHILDREN LISTED THE NATURAL OR LEGALLY ADOPTED CHILDREN OF THE CONTRIBUTOR? ☐ Yes ☐ No If no, indicate each child who is not on a separate sheet of paper.

ISP 1300 (4-90)

22.	ARE ANY OF THE CHILDREN LISTED RECEIVING OR HAVE THEY APPLIED FOR BENEFITS UNDER:	A. THE CANADA PENSION PLAN? ☐ Yes ☒ No	B. THE QUEBEC PENSION PLAN? ☐ Yes ☒ No	If yes, indicate which children and under which Social Insurance Number on a separate sheet of paper.
23.	ARE ALL OF THE CHILDREN LISTED STILL IN YOUR CUSTODY AND CONTROL?	☒ Yes ☐ No	If no, indicate each child who is not and give the date each child ceased to be in your custody and control on a separate sheet of paper.	
24.	HAVE YOU BEEN WHOLLY OR SUBSTANTIALLY MAINTAINING ALL OF THE CHILDREN LISTED SINCE THE DEATH OF THE CONTRIBUTOR?	☒ Yes ☐ No	If no, explain on a separate sheet of paper.	

SECTION D — INFORMATION ABOUT THE APPLICANT IF OTHER THAN THE SURVIVING SPOUSE NAMED IN SECTION B OR IF SECTION B IS BLANK

25.	MR., MRS., ETC.	GIVEN NAME AND INITIAL		FAMILY NAME				
26.	HOME ADDRESS	(Number and Street)		(Apt. No., P.O. Box, R.R. No.)	TYPE NM ADR	FOREIGN CODE	LANG.	
27.	(City, Town or Village)	(Province or Territory)	(Country)	(Postal Code)	CONS. CODE	NO. LNS	A.L.	

ATTACH A SEPARATE SHEET OF PAPER EXPLAINING WHY YOU ARE MAKING THIS APPLICATION.

SECTION E — DECLARATION OF THE APPLICANT

28. I declare that, to the best of my knowledge and belief, the information given in this application is true and complete and I undertake to notify the Income Security Programs Branch of any changes in circumstances that may affect eligibility for benefits.

DECLARATION OF WITNESS REQUIRED ONLY WHEN APPLICANT SIGNS BY MARK

I have read the contents of this application to the applicant who appeared fully to understand them and who made his or her mark in my presence.

SIGNATURE OF APPLICANT ▶ *Mary M. Smith*

SIGNATURE OF WITNESS

DATE OF APPLICATION
Day 1 5 | Month 0 3 | Year 9 1

Note: Signature by mark (X) is acceptable if witnessed by any responsible person who must complete the declaration opposite.

ADDRESS OF WITNESS

TELEPHONE NUMBER

TELEPHONE NUMBER

IT IS AN OFFENCE TO MAKE A FALSE OR MISLEADING STATEMENT IN THIS APPLICATION.

OFFICE USE ONLY — DO NOT WRITE BELOW THIS LINE

BENEFIT INFORMATION
ACTION BNFT AL B/C D E F G S | | | | 0,0 | C.P.P. NUMBER | APR REC'D D M Y | OT. EFF. M Y | CHILD SONC | EA

ACCESS CODE ACTION BNFT | OT EFF M Y | CHILD SONC | MISCELLANEOUS 1 (OLD) (NEW) | MISCELLANEOUS 2 (NEW) | B/C D | NUMBER OF LINES E F G S | | 0,0 0,0 | EC

MONETARY INFO
CODE | CHILD SONC | RECOVERY BNFT CHILD | SIGN | UNDER/OVPYMNT | ACCRUED RECOVERY CPP | OT. EFF. OPP M Y | CPP WITHHOLD ARREARS RATE | OPP WITHHOLD ARREARS RATE | FA
| | | | | | | | | FA
| | | | | | | | | FA
TOTAL ▶ | | | | | | | | FB

EARNINGS
YR | TYPE | PLAN | CATEGORY | EARNINGS | CONTRIBUTIONS | TOTAL EARNINGS | CONTRIBUTIONS | GA
| | | | | | | | GE

DATE APPLICATION RECEIVED

Application taken by:

Application approved pursuant to Subsection 59(3) of the Canada Pension Plan.

Date

Effective Date _____

Authorized Signature

	DATE	TYPE OF REJECT	BATCH NO.	CYCLE	DATE	SIGNATURE
1						
2						

GLOSSARY

ADMINISTRATOR

Individual appointed by the court to administer the estate of a person who dies without a will. Also known as an estate trustee, or personal representative.

AFFIDAVIT

Statement of fact sworn before a lawyer or notary public

BENEFICIARY

A person who derives some benefit, whether money or property, from the will of a deceased person

CAPITAL GAIN

Profit realized on the sale of an asset or the profit deemed to be realized as if the asset had been sold at the time of the owner's death

CAPITAL LOSS

Loss experienced on the sale of an asset or the loss deemed to be realized as if the asset had been sold at the time of the owner's death

CERTIFICATE OF APPOINTMENT OF ESTATE TRUSTEE WITH A WILL

The term used by the Ontario Court for the court grant confirming the appointment of an estate trustee or executor named in the will and confirming the validity of the will itself.

CERTIFICATE OF APPOINTMENT OF ESTATE TRUSTEE WITHOUT A WILL

The term used by the Ontario Court for the court grant appointing an estate trustee to administer the estate of an individual dying intestate.

CODICIL

An amendment to a will requiring all the formalities of execution needed for a will

ENCROACH

The act of paying out to the beneficiary portions of the money or other assets being held for that beneficiary in trust

ESCHEAT

The process by which the assets of a deceased person pass to the provincial government when he or she dies without a will and without a spouse and next-of-kin

ESTATE TRUSTEE

Individual appointed in a will to administer the estate of the deceased, or where there is no will, and individual who applies for and is granted a Certificate of Appointment of Estate Trustee. Also referred to as a personal representative.

EXECUTE A WILL

Technical term for signing your will in front of witnesses or without witnesses if it is a holograph will; doing all acts necessary to give it legal effect

HOLOGRAPH WILL

A will written completely in the handwriting of the person making it, having no witnesses to the signature of the person making it

INTESTATE

Either the act of dying without a will or the person who dies without a will

ISSUE

Descendants of a person, including not only children but grandchildren, great-grandchildren, and more remote descendants

LEGACY

Property or money given by a will

LIFE INTEREST

A benefit given to a beneficiary in a will which permits that beneficiary to enjoy or have the use of some property or some amount of money for the balance of the beneficiary's lifetime only

NEXT-OF-KIN

Blood relatives of a person dying intestate who inherit by reason of the Succession Law Reform Act

NOTARIZED OR NOTARIAL COPY

True copy of an original document certified by a lawyer or notary public as being a true copy

ONTARIO COURT (GENERAL DIVISION)

The court which is responsible for the appointment of personal representatives and generally involved with problems arising during the administration of estates

PERSONAL PROPERTY

All property with the exception of real estate and buildings; also known as "personalty" (as opposed to "real property" or "realty")

PERSONAL REPRESENTATIVE

The individual administering an estate. Also known as an Estate Trustee.

PER STIRPES

A method of dividing assets of an estate such that if a member of the group among which the assets are being divided happens to be dead at the time of the division, the children of that deceased member of the group will divide among them the share that their parent would have received had he or she been alive

REAL PROPERTY

Land and buildings; also known as "real estate" or "realty"

RESIDUARY BENEFICIARY

The beneficiary to whom the residue of the estate is left

RESIDUE

That portion of an estate remaining after all specific bequests and specific devises have been made

SPECIFIC BEQUEST

A gift under a will of a specific item of personal property or a specific amount of cash

SPECIFIC DEVISE

A gift under a will of a specific item of real property

TESTATOR

A man who makes a will; feminine form — "testatrix"

TRANSMISSION

Transfer of property to beneficiary after probate of will or Letters of Administration obtained

WILL

The legal statement of a person's wishes concerning the disposal of his or her property after death

If you have enjoyed this book and would like to receive a free catalogue of all Self-Counsel titles, please write to:

Self-Counsel Press
1481 Charlotte Road
North Vancouver BC V7J 1H1

Or visit us on the World Wide Web at
http://www.self-counsel.com